ROMAN

LIFE

100 B.C. TO A.D. 200

by John R. Clarke

New photography
by Michael Larvey

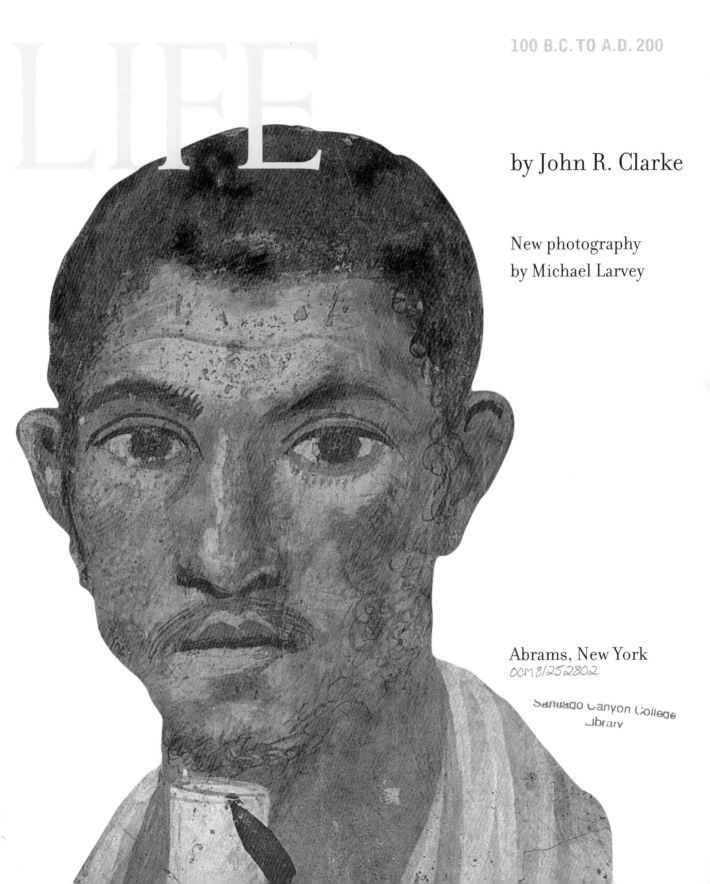

Abrams, New York

CONTENTS

ACKNOWLEDGMENTS

First and foremost, I wish to thank Michael Larvey for his many fine photographs. This book would have not come about without his encouragement and that of Lindley Kirksey Young. I am also most grateful to the friends who read the manuscript, offering suggestions for revision and correcting errors: Andrew Riggsby, Anthony Corbeill, Marcos Jimenez, and Roger Ulrich. Special thanks are due to Onur Öztürk, for his digital drawings and reconstructions, and to Russell Hassell, who designed the book. Thanks go to Aiah R. Wieder at Abrams for her able editorial assistance.

The staff of the Division of Instructional Innovation and Assessment at the University of Texas worked tirelessly to make the CD-ROM that accompanies this book a reality: Coco Kishi, Suzanne Rhodes, and especially Scott Herrick. Special thanks go to James Packer and John Berge for their digital reconstructions of the Forum of Trajan, and to Jane Whitehead for her drawings. I am also most grateful to the individuals who facilitated work at archaeological sites and museums in Italy: Pietro Giovanni Guzzo (Pompeii); Stefano De Caro, Mariá Luisa Nava, and Maria Rosaria Boriello (Naples); Emilia Talamo (Rome); Anna Gallina Zevi and Jane Shepherd (Ostia); Adele Campanelli (Chieti).

Finally, I wish to thank Margaret L. Kaplan, an extraordinary editor, who guided this project with great skill and understanding.

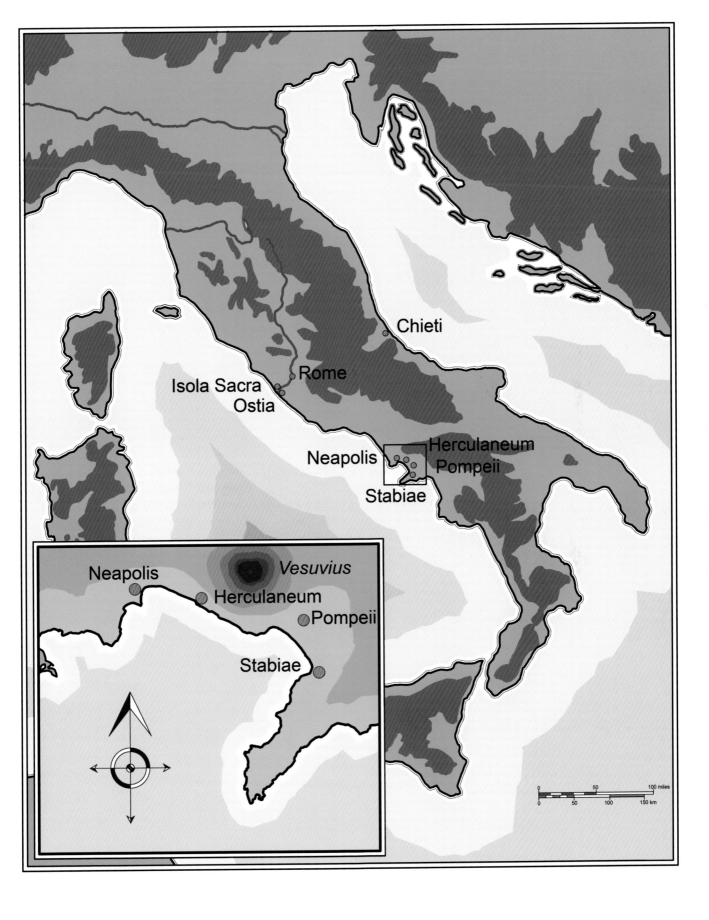

Chieti

Rome

Isola Sacra
Ostia

Neapolis   Herculaneum
                  Pompeii

        Stabiae

Neapolis   *Vesuvius*
            Herculaneum

                Pompeii

        Stabiae

0 50   100 miles
0 50 100 150 km

INTRODUCTION

This book is my best answer to a seemingly simple question: "What was life like in ancient Roman times?" To answer this question is not such a simple matter. First of all, we have to ask "Whose life?" because life—then as today—was quite different for people of different social classes. Differences among ancient Romans multiply if we take into consideration the huge slave population, not to mention the important social class of former slaves or freedpersons. Life in the country was quite different from life in the cities, and life in the capital, Rome, was different from life in all the other cities of the Roman Empire. How to express these differences in how people lived their lives?

In my thirty-five years of teaching and writing about the Romans living between 100 B.C. and A.D. 200, I have taken many approaches. Wearing my art historian's cap, I have focused on visual art; wearing my archaeologist's hard hat, I've emphasized ancient digs at Pompeii, Rome, and Ostia. Despite the pleasures of exploring the meaning of beautiful and often strange artworks, or the thrill of discovering new artifacts and dating them, neither art history nor archaeology alone can bring ancient Romans to life. In this book I have

begun—not with the art or the archaeology —but with Roman people. I have written little stories about individuals whom I have come to know. These are real people who lived some 2,000 years ago. I follow them as they sacrifice to the gods, go to work, take in a play at the theater, stop at a local tavern for a drink, visit the local baths, plan a dinner party, or even bury their best friend. It's because of the work of archaeologists and experts on inscriptions that we have the names of these individuals, as well as an amazing amount of information about their social status, relative wealth, ethnic origins, and professions. These are the Romans whose lives you will follow as you read this book.

Now and then I have had to invent individuals—usually characters who are secondary to one of my little stories. I have assigned them names appropriate for their social status and place of origin. When these made-up characters appear, their names are printed in *italic type* the first time I use them.

To fill out these real-life stories, I also present a number of images with fairly detailed explanations. These images with "rich captions" are meant to expand and complicate the discussion a bit, presenting, for example, other religious practices from those that the individual in the story is carrying out. Finally, the CD-ROM, *The House of the Vettii, Pompeii: An Interactive Visit* is an invitation to explore—on your own—the life of the ancient Roman house. Since the house was a place for worship, business, and entertainment, its spaces and their decoration are quite foreign to our modern notions of the home. Since you have to assume a social role (slave, client, guest, or family member) to navigate the CD-ROM, you will begin to think like an ancient Roman—especially as you begin to explore the complex and beautiful mythological paintings in the entertainment rooms.

"Just Like Us?"

One of the main aims of this book is to ask in what ways the ancient Romans were like us. It is not an idle question, since so much of European and American culture looks back to ancient Rome for models. Many things that we take for granted come from ancient Rome. A short list includes measurement systems (in the United States, for example, inches, feet, and miles), grammar, writing (we use the Roman alphabet), words (about one-third of the words in the English language come from Latin; nearly all the words in Romance languages come from Latin), law, and the concepts of democracy and monarchy. Paradoxically, these two seemingly opposed systems of government, the democratic state and the empire, both come from Rome. In the Renaissance, princes and would-be monarchs modeled themselves on the Roman Emperors (27 B.C.–A.D. 327). The idea of empire played out in many theaters from the Renaissance to the present, including Mussolini's project to found a new Roman Empire through fascism. Yet in the time of the American and French Revolutions, it was the ancient Roman Republic (450–27 B.C.) that inspired the likes of Thomas Jefferson and Napoleon.

Because of this long Euro-American tradition of studying and emulating the ancient Romans, most introductions to Roman civilization emphasize the many ways in which the ancient Romans were just like us. But there is a price to be paid for taking this approach, because so much of what we know comes from classical literature, written by elite men. Naturally, these texts give us the mind-set of the upper classes of Roman society. There's not a single woman writer, nor are there any literary texts written by slaves, former slaves, or freeborn workers.

To reconstruct the lives and identities of the other 98 percent of ancient Romans, we have to rely upon the kind of evidence you find in this book: inscriptions on tombs, graffiti, and shop signs. What emerges is a much livelier and multifaceted society than you get from reading Cicero or Virgil. The quirks and idiosyncrasies that take visual and verbal expression among the lower classes reveal a host of ways of dealing with life. In particular, if we look at buildings and artworks in well-preserved archaeological sites (like, for instance, the miraculously preserved House of the Vettii at Pompeii, or the Forum of the Corporations at Ostia), we start to understand how ancient Romans dealt with the practices of everyday life—everything from birth to death: religion, work, bathing, recreation, drinking, dining, and so on.

You be the judge. Were the ancient Romans just like us? If you keep this question in mind as you read this book, you might come up with some surprising answers.

I

LIFE WITH THE GODS

The city of Rome is buzzing with excitement. The Emperor Augustus himself is going to inaugurate the new Altar of Peace (Ara Pacis), erected by the Senate to celebrate his safe return from Spain and Gaul—and his military victories there. In a brilliant strategic move, Augustus has refused the usual triumphal arch. Instead, he has commissioned artists to design an altar to promote an idea made into a new goddess. She's called Peace (fig. 1). But it's not just the goddess Peace who's celebrated. It also celebrates Augustus—not as a military leader but as the man who brought back old-time religion. Everything on the altar promotes this idea.

It's a holiday for everyone, from slaves to Senators—men, women, and children. And there's something for everyone over on the Field of Mars. Many can remember when it was little more than a huge, muddy field for mustering the army. Now it's an enormous, open plaza paved with marble and dominated by a huge obelisk from Egypt that serves as the pointer for a sundial (figs. 2 and 3). That pointer caused a bit of a stir on Augustus's birthday, September 23, because on that day its shadow struck the entrance to the Altar of Peace. Today, of course, the shadow is marking a different season. Some people are examining the enormous solar clock, learning how to read the time of day and the positions of the constellations on the glittering white marble pavement, where bronze letters spell out in Greek the time and season. Farther to the north is Augustus' mausoleum, a huge

2 BELOW The Field of Mars, with the Augustan monuments.
A. Mausoleum
B. Sundial
C. Obelisk
D. Ara Pacis

3 BELOW, RIGHT Drawing of the Augustan Altar of Peace with the sundial and mausoleum

4 OPPOSITE Augustan Altar of Peace, Rome. Detail of the south processional frieze

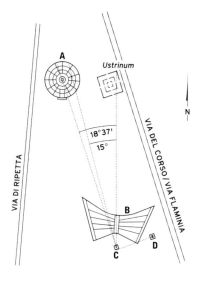

cylinder with a mounded top—slated to be the final resting place for the ashes of Augustus and all his family. But almost everyone is heading for the Altar of Peace, just alongside the via Flaminia, the main road going due north from the city center.

The altar marks the spot where Augustus sacrificed to the gods in thanksgiving for his safe return from Spain and Gaul in the summer of 13 B.C. Then, a portable altar had been set up, surrounded by a wooden enclosure. Today, Augustus will reenact that sacrifice and perform rites to inaugurate the permanent Altar of Peace on that same spot.

Porcia and her husband, the Senator *Marcus Claudius Rufus*, arrive in sedan chairs carried by hefty slaves who double as bodyguards. They immediately fix their eyes on the frieze carved along the marble wall enclosing the altar. It shows Augustus himself, surrounded by priests and bodyguards and followed by his whole clan (fig. 4). It's the shock of recognition that makes Porcia grasp Marcus' arm: There's Agrippa at the head of the family—Augustus' right-hand man and his son-in-law. Sadly, he died before the sculptors completed the frieze, leav-

ing Julia a widow. Julia looks out, and right next to her is the most important woman in Rome: Augustus' wife Livia, Julia's stepmother.

Speculation begins. Who will succeed Augustus? After all, it's obvious to Porcia and Marcus—and anyone belonging to the elite classes (Senators and equestrians)—that Augustus is founding a hereditary dynasty. Although he constantly protests that he is simply the "first citizen" (*princeps*), it is clear that both the common people and the elites want peace and prosperity. It seems that the only way to continue without civic strife is to accept the fact: The Republic is over. Augustus has founded the Roman Empire.

Porcia calls Marcus, who is puzzling over just which of the children of Augustus' family are depicted on the south frieze, to come over to the wall on the north (fig. 5). She's found a procession of priests and Senators here, with Marcus himself among them, marching along in his toga, with more of Augustus' family at the end of the procession. How clever! It all makes sense. Porcia explains it in an instant. This is the "political" side of the altar—and it's dedicated to the Senate. Augustus does not appear here.

Agrippa   Julia   Livia

5 RIGHT Augustan Altar of
Peace, Rome. Detail of the
north processional frieze

6 OPPOSITE Augustan Altar of
Peace, Rome. Detail of the west
side, the Sacrifice of Aeneas

He's on the other side, surrounded by priests with his head veiled with the edge of his toga. He's showing everyone his favorite role, as high priest of Rome, *pontifex maximus*.

The movement of the crowd and the bellowing of the sacrificial heifers tell Porcia and Marcus that it's time to take their places before the altar. They veil their heads and turn silent, even while congratulating themselves on figuring out the messages of two processional friezes. Looking up, they see the reliefs that face them on either side of the door to the altar itself (fig. 6). On the right there's an image of Aeneas sacrificing. Just like Augustus at the head of the family procession around the corner to the right, Aeneas has his head veiled as he sacrifices in thanksgiving for finally landing in Italy after his long and dangerous journey from Troy.

Porcia and Marcus have just been to a reading of Virgil's new epic, commissioned by Augustus' wealthy friend Maecenas. Virgil calls it *The Aeneid*, but Marcus calls it pure propaganda, for Virgil makes it clear that Aeneas is Augustus' ancestor. Since Aeneas' mother was none other than the goddess Venus, this means that Augustus is the descendant of a goddess. And if Aeneas escapes from burning Troy with the statues of the city's protector deities (the *Penates*), it's so that he can come to Italy and found the new Troy: Rome. Just as Aeneas founded Rome, so

Augustus restores it. And if Aeneas was anything, he was respectful of the gods and family. Just as Aeneas showed his piety to the gods by sacrificing at Lavinium, so Augustus demonstrates his piety for all to see on the altar dedicated to Peace. A very neat package—and one that ignores the bloody facts of Augustus' rise to power.

There's a flurry of excitement as the *real* Augustus arrives, looking a little older than his likeness in the relief, but surrounded by a similar entourage of bodyguards carrying their ceremonial staffs (the *fasces*, made of birch rods bound together around an axe) and by the priests. Marcus and Porcia recognize men they know among the priests.

While Marcus and Porcia consider their good fortune at being among the best people and in the front row, *Gaius* and *Silvia* arrive on foot with their three children in tow. They have to push their way through the crowd of ordinary people who have followed the processions of Senators and equestrians with their armies of slaves—all to see this

new wonder of Rome. They've come up the via Flaminia from the crowded Subura neighborhood where they now live. Gaius sighs, thinking of their little farmhouse out in the rolling hills of northern Latium. If they hadn't been forced out by the henchmen of a certain wealthy Senator, Gaius and his family would still be there: poor farmers on their own little plot of land. Now they are all crammed into a firetrap of an apartment building—on the fifth floor, right under the rafters—and depend on the city for doles of grain. As a freeborn citizen Gaius can vote, and Augustus keeps the grain doles coming to keep his citizen-voters happy. Or relatively so.

True, there are many holidays like this one to get the family out of their miserable quarters—and Gaius out of the shop where he spends his hours making simple furniture for little pay. A slave of one of these rich people could be far more fortunate—and wealthy.

In front of them they see a knot of people stepping down from the via Flaminia to inspect the altar. Many, like Gaius, wear togas. They are freeborn citizens, and Augustus requires them to wear the heavy, unwieldy white wool garment at public functions like these. Wives of freeborn citizens must wear the stola—the equivalent of the man's toga. All the rest—slaves and foreigners—wear far more practical clothing for a cold day like this. Some of the men wear leggings and hooded cloaks; the women wear colorful dresses draped over long tunics. There's a great variety of headgear as well.

At last, Gaius and his family get to the back of the altar. It is simply astonishing, for by some magic the sculptor has cov-

ered the entire enclosure wall with every vine and every flower they knew in the country (fig. 7). Fantastic acanthus scrolls turn into other plants: laurel, ivy, and vines with grape clusters. There are acanthus flowers, roses, and poppies. There's even a sprig of oak. Yet more astonishing are all the living creatures that fill the carved space. Swans top the exuberant vegetation, but many smaller creatures are hidden within the foliage (fig. 8). Already, little *Cassius* is playing a game with his sisters, seeing how many snakes, lizards, and birds they can find.

Silvia admires the relief above: a beautiful woman holding twin boys (fig. 9). The one to the right plays with fruit gathered in his mother's lap, the other reaches for her breast. To either side are two women, one riding a swan, the other a mythical sea dragon, their cloaks billowing around their bodies. Around the sea dragon Silvia notices waves, but beneath the swan she sees an overturned *amphora*, a storage vessel with two handles,

pouring out sweet water on marsh grass. And beneath the beautiful woman in the center is dry land on which a cow rests, watching a sheep graze. All this reminds Silvia of their farm in the country.

She thinks she understands what the picture means. The woman is Italy. The women with billowing cloaks are the Winds. The Wind on the sea dragon symbolizes the oceans that surround Italy, while the Wind carried by the swan stands for the land. Somehow, it all comes clear to Silvia; she is, after all, like this beautiful woman with her twins, a freeborn Roman woman rearing her children and enjoying the bounty of Italy—even if she must live away from the land.

It is time for the sacrifice to begin. The drone of double pipes and the chanting of prayers silence the crowd, while a procession looking much like the one on the south wall appears. Augustus leads, his head veiled. The priests and body-guards surround him, and the sacrificial animals follow: two white heifers, their horns gilded and bedecked with flowers, and a white ewe. Brawny, bare-chested men wearing kilt-like garments handle the bellowing cows and the bleating sheep. Three more men in similar dress hold large mallets; others hold triangular knives. The moment to sacrifice the animals arrives. Mallets go up in unison and come down with a heavy thud, stunning the animals. They fall to the gleaming marble pavement. It soon turns crimson as the priests cut the animals' throats, gathering blood in shallow dishes. They gut the heifers and the ewe, pulling out the livers and entrails. As Augustus ascends the steps to pour some of the blood on the altar, a diviner (*haruspex*)

inspects the livers for omens. All are good, as everyone expects. Now that the gods have been appeased, long hymns of thanksgiving follow.

The tone lightens as criers announce that Augustus will give the people a public feast in the afternoon. Many more beasts have been slaughtered, and there will be abundant roasted beef and lamb, and plenty to drink for all free citizens of the city.

The Ward-Captains' Altar

A.D. 2

It is a great day for Publius Clodius—perhaps even better than the day he won his freedom from his master, Publius. Today he and three of his friends—former slaves like himself—will perform their first public sacrifice as ward captains. Publius wears a newly woven toga as he walks with his family to the street crossing that defines his city ward. Publius will do what Augustus did eleven years earlier: inaugurate an altar with a special sacrifice. This altar is much more modest than the Altar of Peace, of course, and in a far more crowded setting. It is only a little over three feet (one meter) high and stands on a low marble base. There is no room for an enclosure wall like the one surrounding the Altar of Peace, but markers define a square around it, and people can see all four sides. A small gable attached to the building behind it will protect the expensive white marble from the elements.

Publius Clodius saw the opportunity to come up in the world when Augustus decided to organize the chaos of Rome by dividing it into fourteen regions with

9 Augustan Altar of Peace, Rome. Detail of the east side, with the goddess Tellus/Italy/Peace

▶ **Finding the Ward-Captains' Altar.**
In 1906, when workmen were digging near the new Garibaldi Bridge, they found a stone altar, miraculously intact, at the depth of twenty-five feet (about eight meters) below the modern via Arenula (fig. 10). They called in the archaeologist Giuseppe Gatti, who found that the altar was still resting on its original travertine base with the inscription (ma)*G*(i)*STRI VICI AESCLETI ANNI VIIII:* "The Ward Captains of the Aesculetus Ward in the Ninth Year (dedicated this altar)." This same inscription appears on the altar itself, along with the names of the four ward captains, or *magistri,* who dedicated it to the Emperor Augustus.

With a little detective work, Gatti was able to identify this particular city ward, or *vicus.* It was one of 265 that Augustus established in 8–7 B.C. in an effort to bring order to a city that had rapidly grown to a population of nearly one million. Even the number *VIIII* (a variant for the Roman IX) was significant; they dedicated the altar on the ninth year since Augustus had established the new post of *vicomagistri,* in A.D. 2.

265 wards (*vici*), and he immediately started campaigning to be appointed a ward captain. He had just bought his freedom and was relatively well off, still making money by overseeing his former master's milling and baking factory. Indeed, he had enough saved to set up his own bakery in the neighborhood, and to increase his political clout by now and again giving out free bread to the citizens of his ward. With all his money, his new status as a freedman, and the good will of his ward, he fully expected to be made a ward captain, but even so, when the Emperor's official invited him to accept the honor, he leapt with joy.

Publius Clodius has arrived at a social standing beyond his wildest dreams as a slave. Together with his three fellow ward captains, he polices and protects the Aesculetus ward. They keep watch over traffic, crime, and fires—but best of all, they can do what Publius is setting off to do today: sacrifice to the Emperor. In the office of *vicomagister*, religion and civic duty merge.

Publius and his neighbors are glad that the good Augustus has recognized the importance of worshipping the Lares. For centuries, street-corner altars to the Lares of the Crossroads have seen offerings of cakes, milk, and an occasional piglet—unofficially. Everyone knows that these twin deities, who also protect one's house,

will protect the streets if appeased properly and regularly. But now it is official, and the Lares have a new feature: they are now the Lares of Augustus—the same twins, but now holding the symbol of the *princeps*, the laurel branch (fig. 11).

When Publius and his fellow *vicomagistri* commissioned the altar, they instructed the sculptor to carve images of the Lares of Augustus on the right and left sides. But as the crowd parts to make way for Publius, it is the image on the front of the altar that he strains to see. Yes! There it is! Publius himself, with his three counterparts stretching their arms over an altar— an image that captures this inaugural sacrifice for all eternity (fig. 12). Now no one will forget Publius, for if they cannot recognize his features (his face *is* rather small), they can read his name carved in big letters above the Lar on the altar's left side. The four had flipped a coin to decide which two would have their names carved on the front, for there is only room for two names between the line that dedicates the altar to the Lares and the line recording the date when they all became *magistri*. Just as well: Instead of having his name crowded on the front with another of the ward captains, Publius has his own space. The inscription reads *P CLODIUS P L:* "Publius Clodius freedman of Publius": his friend Salvius, freedman of Lucius,

10 OPPOSITE Altar of the Vicomagistri of the Vicus Aesculetus, Rome

11 ABOVE Altar of the Vicomagistri of the Vicus Aesculetus, Rome. Detail showing Lar

has his own space above the Lar on the right-hand side.

The altar also shows the special sacrifice that the ward captains will perform today. In addition to the pig—the usual animal offered to the Lares—they will offer a bull. The bull is for the Emperor, making this sacrifice much more costly and complex than the ones that Publius performs at home—usually just an offering of cakes and wine, at most a piglet.

Publius realizes that the sculptor had to cut corners a bit to fit everything in. He has made the *victimarii*, the bare-chested men who handle and kill the animals—as well as the animals themselves—much

smaller than normal. The *victimarii* crouch down in front of the altar to keep Publius and his fellow *vicomagistri* in clear sight. The *victimarius* on the left, wearing only a kilt, carries the sacrificial mallet for stunning the animals over his left shoulder. He restrains the pig with a leash and, like his partner, seems to be kneeling.

Publius doesn't mind this bit of artistic license, since it allowed the sculptor to play up the importance of the *vicomagistri* and to include critical details like the laurel crowns on their heads. Everyone knows that laurel—sacred to Apollo and used to crown a triumphant

Some ward officials were slaves.
During construction work on the Caelian Hill in 1906, excavators uncovered an altar that names another *vicus,* the one of Statae Matris. It commemorates the sixth year of the establishment of the office of ward captains, and bears the names of the four officials—called *ministri* rather than *magistri*: Felix, Florus, Eudoxsus, and Polyclitus, all of them still slaves. In addition to their names (which incorporate the names of their owners), these four *vicoministri* made sure that the artist included the year and date of the altar's dedication—September 18, 2 B.C. and the names of the consuls at the time: L. Caninius Gallus and C. Fufius Geminus.

Despite all these inscriptions, the altar is plainer than the one from the *vicus Aesculetus,* with no human figures. Instead, the oak crown, symbol of civic virtue, appears on the front, with laurel branches on the sides—substitutes for figures of the *lares.* On the back is a libation bowl. Despite its pared-down decoration—indication of the leaner purses of the men who paid for it—the altar demonstrates how important it was to Augustus to enlist the piety and loyalty of the slaves in Rome.

12 Altar of the Vicomagistri of the Vicus Aesculetus, Rome. Detail of the sacrificial scene

general—is one of Augustus' emblems. They had insisted that the sculptor show their facial features even though he had to crowd all four of the ward captains around the altar, performing the sacrifice together with their togas drawn over their heads (just like Augustus on his Altar of Peace). Publius recognizes himself on the left, behind Salvius, who is pouring a libation from a small libation bowl (*patera*). He and the other two ward captains extend their hands to sprinkle pinches of incense on the flames.

It is a pity that the sculptor didn't have enough room to include both of the bodyguards to which Publius and his fellow *vicomagistri* are entitled. There's only one, over at the left edge of the altar, but everyone can recognize him because he's carrying the *fasces*—just like the guards accompanying Augustus on the Altar of Peace. Publius is pleased with how the altar came out—except for one detail. Why did the sculptor have to put the double-pipe player right in the middle? And why is he so large? Although he's important to the sacrifice, he didn't pay for it! With this thought in mind, Publius hears the drone of the pipes, pulling him from the image to the reality. The sacrifice is about to begin.

Early Morning in the Slave Quarters of the House of the Vettii

A.D. 79

On a clear August dawn in the little town of Pompeii, workers are making their way up the slopes of Vesuvius to trim the grapevines. They can see the island of Capri on the far side of the sparkling blue Bay of Naples. Down in the town, a servant wakes Aulus Vettius Restitutus. Today, he will offer sacrifice in the servants' atrium before receiving his clients in the official part of his house. His brother, Aulus Vettius Conviva, is away in Rome on an important mission. The Emperor's agents have informed him that he will finally become a *sevir Augustalis*, the highest rank a former slave can attain. Conviva has devoted his money and his energies to becoming an Augustalis, for this recognition will go much further than anything else can to remove the stain of former slavery from their children. Perhaps their offspring will become city officials or priests—routes to glory closed to freedmen, even wealthy freedmen like themselves.

Restitutus drinks a cup of hot water in bed, then washes rapidly (he'll have a proper bath after business hours). He dons his toga and makes his way from his bedroom, which is tucked away behind the big reception spaces off the peristyle, through the huge atrium, and into the much more modest atrium that is the center of the servants' quarters.

Syriacus, his jovial cook, is the first to greet him. Conviva and Restitutus spent considerable time and money to acquire Syriacus, and the splendid dishes he concocts are reward enough for their

trouble. They were so pleased with a banquet featuring a roasted pig stuffed with sausages and grilled dormice that they promised to redecorate his room in any style he liked. As it turned out, Syriacus was most impressed by the paintings in the local brothel, so the Vettii brothers obliged him and found a painter to decorate the room next to the kitchen with three pictures of couples making love (see CD-ROM).

But it's a big painting in the well-lit servants' atrium that Syriacus, Restitutus, and the small army of slaves are looking at right now (fig. 13). It shows a man in a toga, its edge pulled over his head, sacrificing to the Lares of the household: they are the twins, dressed in kilts, who raise their drinking horns with one arm to squirt wine into the pails they carry at their sides. A huge snake, the so-called good spirit (*agathodaemon*), coils his way through the greenery at the bottom of the picture to inspect the offerings on the altar. As Restitutus and the assembled household know, the man in the toga is the guardian spirit (*genius*) of the Vettii clan. The sacrifice that Restitutus will perform this morning is to both the *genius*, who will ensure the fertility and long life of the clan, and to the Lares, who will protect the house and its occupants.

One servant brings a box of incense, another the libation bowl, yet another today's offering: the first fruits of the brothers' orchard. One of the slaves plays the double pipes well, and so the sacrifice—and the day—officially begins.

13 House of the Vettii, Pompeii. The painted Lararium in the servants' atrium

◄ ▲ **Sutoria Primigenia's Kitchen Lararium.** The unusual *Lararium* in the House of Sutoria Primigenia in Pompeii decorates a tiny kitchen and shows the whole household attending a sacrifice (figs. 14 and 15). Large figures of the Lares frame the scene. Next in size are the figures of the *genius*, accompanied by the *juno*, or guardian spirit of the woman of the house—Sutoria herself. Only the *genius* wears the toga, and because

he is sacrificing, he has pulled its edge over his head. The *juno* wears the proper garment of a Roman matron, the *stola*. To the right are thirteen members of the *familia*, facing outward and wearing white tunics with short sleeves. All of them hold their right arms to their chests, except for the first person at the left in the front row standing near the *genius:* He must be the attendant who carries the incense box.

14 OPPOSITE House of Sutoria Primigenia, Pompeii. The north and east walls of the kitchen

15 ABOVE House of Sutoria Primigenia, Pompeii. Detail of the east wall of the kitchen

◀ ▼ **A Garden Lararium.** The owner of this small house made the Lararium the focus of his garden, paying an artist to construct a shrine placed so that it can be seen from the front entrance and packing it with as many features as his imagination—and purse—would allow (figs. 16 and 17). The Lararium stands upon a cement podium surrounded by a canal that must have been filled with water. The *genius* stands at the back of the vault on a plant-covered base pouring a libation on a round altar. He holds a cornucopia over his left shoulder.

But where are the Lares? When the excavators uncovered the Lararium, they found two statues of Lares, along with a lamp and a bowl, under the shelter of the niche. These objects, all in bronze, must have been the treasures of this modest household (fig. 18). Since wealthy houses often had fountains in the place where this Lararium stands, the owner had the painter create a "water feature" in the guise of a personification of Pompeii's own Sarnus River. There are also two men in a boat on the river, with pack mules at either side of a bridge and scenes of weighing and inspecting baskets of some foodstuff, perhaps onions.

▶ **This scene, from the "Mysteries Room"** of a large villa just north of Pompeii, shows the beginning of a narrative told in a painted frieze with nearly life-size figures (fig. 19). A woman dressed in street clothes seems to ignore the mother attending to her son, who reads from a scroll. A pregnant woman with a laurel crown carries a silver tray laden with cakes. She looks out at the viewer. The dominant image in the frieze—not shown here—is that of the god Dionysus resting in the lap of his consort Ariadne. All of the mortal participants in the proceeding—except for the small boy with the scroll—are women, leading many scholars to conclude that this was a room reserved for women devoted to the cult of Dionysus.

At the Temple of Isis

A.D. 79

Corelia Celsa and her husband, Numerius Popidius Ampliatus, got up even earlier than Restitutus to attend the daybreak ceremonies at the Temple of Isis in Pompeii. They are fervent devotees of the goddess, and proved their devotion by restoring the entire temple after the earthquake that occurred almost seventeen years earlier (fig. 20).

Corelia and Numerius arrive just as the high priest enters the side door of the temple. They hear him unlocking the big double doors at the top of the stairs, then watch as the doors slowly open to reveal white linen curtains hung across them. Now the gatekeeper opens the gate of the court that gives onto the street, and throngs of devotees stream in to take their places alongside Corelia and Numerius in front of the temple. At this point, the high priest draws aside the curtains so that everyone can see the image of Isis. As Numerius intones his special prayer to the goddess, Corelia shakes a beautiful silver-and-gilt rattle called a sistrum, forming a rhythmic chorus to the droning of the pipes and horns. Gradually the music dies down, and only the murmur of prayers remains. An hour passes. Then the priest leads the devotees in greeting the newly risen sun. Numerius and Corelia linger over their devotions while the courtyard slowly empties. For most of the devotees, it is time to begin the day's work.

Many will return at two o'clock, when the shops close and people take their main meals, for the adoration of the holy water. The high priest, in white garments and with shaved head, will descend the stairs of the Purgatorium to draw some of the sacred water brought from the Nile that is stored there (fig. 21). He will then ascend the steps of the temple to lead the devotees in their worship of this water, sacred to Isis.

Although Corelia and Numerius will return for the water devotion, they are in no hurry to return home now; their trusted slaves and freedmen will take care of Numerius' many enterprises in Pompeii and beyond, and Corelia has plenty of help with the house and the children. As the couple strolls around the freshly decorated peristyle, they reminisce about the terrible earthquake that reduced this temple to ruins. Numerius, already a successful merchant, had married Corelia, his young and beautiful ex-slave, two years earlier, and their first son was just a toddler. Numerius, himself an ex-slave, decided then and there to put all his resources into restoring the temple. Going before the city council (the decurions), whose permission he needed to carry out the work, he made an unusual request. He would pay for the rebuilding of the temple, but his son, Numerius Popidius Celsinus, was to receive credit—and a seat on the city council. After some heated

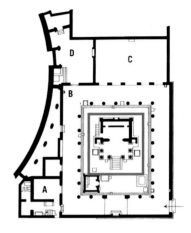

20 OPPOSITE Temple of Isis, Pompeii. Hypothetical reconstruction

21 ABOVE Temple of Isis, Pompeii. Plan
A. Purgatorium
B. Statue of Bacchus
C. Assembly hall
D. Initiation room

◀ **A Ceremony of the Cult of Isis.**
Adoration of the Sacred Water
(fig. 22). Two priests and a priestess
stand in the portico of the temple,
the one in the middle holding a
vessel containing holy water from
the Nile. The flanking priest and
the priestess shake sistra. Another
priest, at the foot of the steps, fans
the flame on the altar. Devotees
stand to right and left, with other
priests, shaking sistra while a
musician at the right front plays
a long flute.

The Six-year-old Decurion.

*N(umerius) Popidius N(umerii)
f(ilius) Celsinus aedem Isidis terrae
motu conlapsum a fundamento
p(ecunia) s(ua) restituit; hunc
decuriones ob liberalitatem, cum
esset annorum sexs, ordini suo
gratis adlegerunt:* "Numerius
Popidius Celsinus, son of Numerius,
rebuilt the Temple of Isis from its
foundation with his own money;
in recognition of his generosity the
decurions admitted him without
cost to their rank—even though
he was only six years of age."

debate, the council agreed, and there,
above the entrance to the court, is proof.
Young Numerius, now eighteen, has
been a city council member since the age
of six. Their money bought a position
for their eldest son that was closed to
Numerius senior no matter how much
money he had, since only freeborn males
can become decurions.

Of course, Numerius saw to it that his
own name appeared within the temple
precinct. In fact, just now he and his wife
are looking at a fine statue of Bacchus
that Numerius had erected in a niche
in the exterior back wall of the temple
(*B* on plan, fig. 21). The inscription says
N. Popidius Ampliatus pater p. s.: "Numerius
Popidius Ampliatus the father set up this
statue at his own expense." In the mosaic
floor of the big assembly hall (*C* on the
plan), Corelia had the mosaicist inscribe
her name, along with those of both her
sons (Numerius Popidius Celsinus and
Numerius Popidius Ampliatus—junior,
named after his father). The couple turns
and enters this room to admire the fancy
center pictures that the talented picture-
painter Titus Hymenaeus persuaded them
to add to the fresco decorations. There
are seven in all, five of them landscapes
with shrines much like those that Titus
painted for their own house, but sprinkled with some Egyptian motifs from his
sketchbook: Egyptian temples, lotuses,

and the like. But Corelia's favorite painting
represents the myth of Io, who ends her
tale of woe in Egypt, where the goddess
Isis receives her (fig. 23).

For Corelia, this is her own story: how
the goddess literally saved her life. She
believes what the high priest told her
after he interpreted her troubled dreams:
that she had literally died, and the life
that she has now is the gift of Isis, who
lengthened her years so that she could
serve the goddess and raise her sons.

Corelia had begun her initiation into
the mysteries of the goddess in this very
hall at the great festival commemorating
the resurrection of Osiris in the ninth
month (November), just twenty years
ago. She remembers her awe at the over-
life-size image of Isis on a pedestal on
the back wall, with marble face, hands,
and feet, but with clothing that was the
work of fine looms and the hands of
many embroiderers. Priests from the
large sanctuary at Puteoli had arrived
with a troupe of sacred mimes. She
already knew the story, but the mime
actors revealed deeper mysteries that
showed Corelia the path to immortality.

In the beginning, Isis, goddess of
heaven, and her brother and husband,
Osiris, rule the world in harmony. Night
falls, and Osiris' evil brother Set—ruler of
darkness—kills Osiris and hacks him into
fourteen pieces. But Isis is pregnant and

23 OPPOSITE Io Landing in Egypt.
Temple of Isis, Pompeii

24 BELOW Celebration of the finding of
the body of Osiris (?), Herculaneum

◀ **Finding the Body of Osiris.** A painting
from an unknown house in Herculaneum
may represent the ceremonies celebrating the finding of the body of Osiris
(fig. 24). A dancer performs before
the open doors of the temple with
musicians behind him, including a
girl playing the cymbals and a woman
beating the tambourine. Priests and
devotees crowd the steps, shaking their
sistra. A burning altar stands in front.
This scene may represent rejoicing
at the resurrection of Osiris—hope of
the devotees of Isis.

gives birth to Horus (Harpocrates), who
is the sun of a new day. Horus avenges
his father's death and rules with Isis
over the living, while Osiris rules over
the dead in the kingdom of the west.

Through this beautiful story Corelia
realized that she—like so many initiates—
could *become* an incarnation of the goddess
and in this way pass on to a blessed existence
after the death of her body. She only has
to win merits enough to appease the judge
who will weigh her soul at the last moment.

After a ritual meal in this very room,
Corelia and the other initiates had entered

the adjoining room through a narrow
door (*D* on plan, fig. 21). It was very dark,
but on the white walls she could make
out images of Isis, Osiris, and Set (called
Typhon by the Greek-speaking devotees),
as well as many animals she could not
identify. The only light came from lamps
suspended from the ceiling, illuminating
the statues with their strange features
and hieroglyphics and the priests who
conducted sacrifices to appease the gods.
The ceremonies, every detail seared into
Corelia's memory, took her slowly and
inexorably to the very door of death.

Although she can never utter the deep
secret that she learned that long night,
she can say this much: "I came to the bor-
ders of death; I walked over the threshold
of Hades; I returned back through all the
stages of life. In the middle of the night
I saw the sun shine brightly; I saw the
gods of heaven and those of Hades, and
I worshiped them face to face"(quoted
from Apuleius, *Metamorphoses*, XI).
This was the dark night of Corelia's soul,
and after this death she was reborn, like
Osiris, grateful to live each additional
day that Isis added to her new life.

A Pine Tree for Attis

A.D. 150

▶ **Ostia, Rome's Supply City**
(fig. 25). The great harbor
Emperor Trajan built in A.D. 100
caused the city to boom, with
warehouses rising by the score
to store the goods that arrived
from all over the Mediterranean,
and multistory, multifamily
apartment buildings to house
20,000 workers and administra-
tors. Ostia had to provision
Rome, a city of over a million
located about fifteen miles up
the Tiber. Note the Field of the
Great Mother (Magna Mater), at
lower center.

Julius Charelampes, priest of the Mother of the Gods of the Colony of Ostia, is hungry and exhausted as he rises to lead—for the nineteenth time in a row—the annual procession of the Tree Bearers. He is forty-eight, and like all the devotees of the Cybele, he has been fasting for a week, since the procession of the Reed Bearers opened the vigil. The day of rejoicing (the *Hilaria*) that ends this period of fasting and sexual abstention is still three days away, but beloved Attis must receive his pine tree today.

Julius breakfasts on a cup of hot water and dons his priestly robes—cut in the Greek manner but with red-striped edges. He hurries to the guild hall of the Tree Bearers, near the field of the Great Mother at the Laurentine Gate. Some of the Tree Bearers have already arrived, wearing short white tunics with a red garment that covers their shoulders and curves down to the knees like an over-sized bib. They go barefoot in deference to the goddess and her beloved, Attis. Today's route is a long one, starting just outside the Roman Gate, where they have built a kind of sledge, a heavy wooden platform supported on wooden rails. It is sturdy enough to hold a handsome umbrella pine, symbol of the dead Attis. They will drag the sledge down the city's principal east–west street, then, after stopping to greet Jupiter at his temple in the Forum, they will tow it south to the Field of the Great Mother. By late after-noon they will place the tree in front of her temple, to await his rebirth after three days and three nights, on March 25.

A throng of devotees follows the solemn procession today, hungry from their fasting and silent in their mourning for Attis. In three days everything will change. These same devotees will feast, drink, sing, and dance in celebration of the Hilaria. There will be games and athletic contests, but first they will parade the Great Mother herself through the streets to the beating of drums, the rattle of tambourines, the clang of cymbals, and the wailing of horns and pipes—the "Phrygian din" that nonbelievers com-plain about. After bringing Cybele back to her temple, Julius and the other priests and priestesses will assist the head of the cult, the Archigallus, in offering a series of sacrifices to initiate the Hilaria, beginning with bloodless offerings and culminating with the sacrifice of a bull.

The three long days have passed. It is the evening of this year's Hilaria, time for the spilling of blood in honor of the goddess, who has resurrected her beloved Attis and in so doing created the fertility of nature and the rebirth of springtime. It was Attis who made the first blood sacrifice, emasculating himself in service to his lover Cybele. In the early days of this ancient cult, a man who wished to be a priest of Cybele would become a eunuch like Attis, cutting off his genitals with a sharp potshard. For this reason, when the Great Mother first came to Rome during the Second Punic War in 191 B.C., her eunuch-priests were confined to her sanctuary on the Palatine Hill, and citizen males could not become priests. All this changed when the Emperor

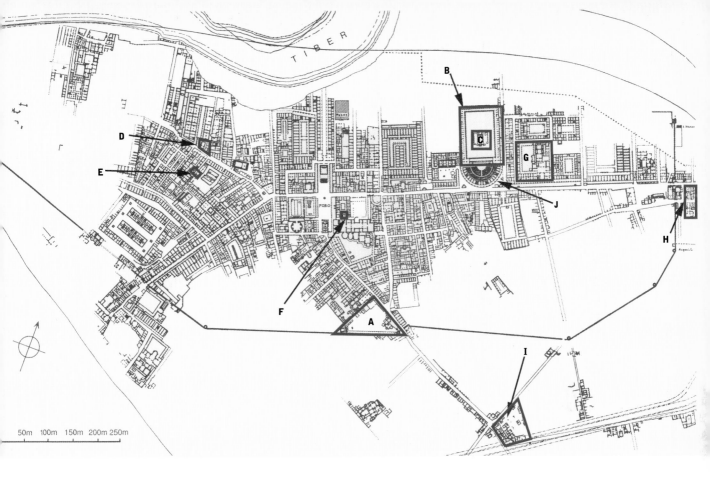

Claudius (ruled A.D. 41–54) opened the priesthood to citizen males who, like Julius himself, were not eunuchs. In place of self-castration, priests and priestesses now cut their arms and legs with knives and offered their blood to Cybele.

Not only one's own blood but also the blood of a bull can purify a devotee and guarantee the goddess's love and protection. Julius surveys the Field and sees several deep trenches covered with sturdy boards with holes bored through them, ready for the *taurobolium*, the sacrifice of a bull. He sees his friend *Aemilia*, a long-time devotee of Cybele, approaching one of the trenches, dressed in a plain white tunic. Today, she will have her second baptism in blood,

exactly twenty years after her first. There is a strong white bull next to the trench; even though its legs are bound, the two handlers have a hard time restraining it. Aemilia descends a ladder into the trench and stretches out on a straw mat, face up, prayers on her lips. The two *victimarii* put the heavy planks back over the trench and pull the struggling animal over it. At a signal given by the officiating priest, one of the *victimarii* stuns the great animal with a heavy mallet blow to the head. One of the two priests in attendance slits the bull's neck while the other makes sure that the bulk of the bull's blood makes its way down through the holes in the planks to bathe Aemilia. The bull's blood will strengthen and purify the initiate. But

since this is Aemilia's second baptism, enacted twenty years after her first, this blood-bath will also give her everlasting happiness.

Julius Charelampes has yet again fulfilled his duties to his mistress and master, the great gods Cybele and her beloved Attis. It is time to return home and rest. He does not know that this will be the last time he fulfills his springtime devotions. Two months later he will die, and his brother, Calpurnius Iovinus, will write on his tomb: "To my dearest brother, Julius Charelampes, priest of the Mother of the Gods of the Colony of Ostia, who led in nineteen trees and lived forty-eight years, two months."

▼ ▶ **The Great Mother on Pompeii's Main Street.** A shop owner on Pompeii's main east–west street commissioned an artist to depict the sacrifice to Cybele at the end of a procession (fig. 26). The four bearers, dressed in white with red bibs hanging from their shoulders, have just set down the bier carrying a huge statue of Cybele (figs. 27 and 28). She wears a dress of deep purple over a white tunic that shows only at the neck and feet. The crown on her head, in the shape of city walls, symbolizes her role as protector of the city. She holds a long golden branch with thin leaves at the top in her left hand and a golden offering plate in her right. In the crook of her left arm she holds a tambourine. The two little lions at her feet symbolize her status as Mistress Over the Animals. Among the large group of devotees, the three principal actors stand out in the front row, all wearing ample white tunics decorated with red stripes. The officiating priest holds out both hands, a little green twig in the right and a gold *patera* in the left.

Dionysus _____

_____

_____ Cybele

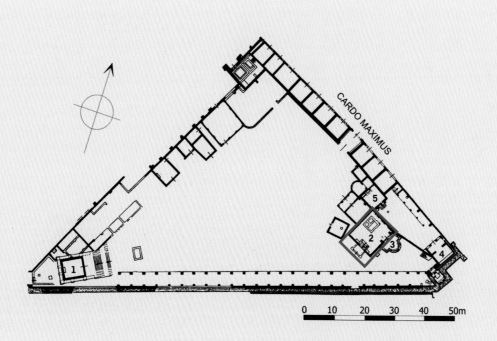

▲ **The Field of Magna Mater, Ostia**
(fig. 29). This large triangle, 48,500
square feet (4,500 square meters), is
bounded by a portion of the southern
city walls at the gate opening to the
Laurentine Road. The Temple of Cybele
(1) occupies the western corner of the
triangle and faces east. A covered
portico surrounds the triangle; the
field was covered with sand to absorb
the blood from the sacrifice of bulls
to the Great Mother. The Sanctuary of
Attis (2) frames the Shrine of Attis (3),
a small building in the western area
that flanks the Temple of Bellona (4)
and the Guild House of the *hastiferi*,
devotees of the cult of the war-goddess
Bellona (5). The main entrance is from
Ostia's north–south thoroughfare, the
Cardo Maximus.

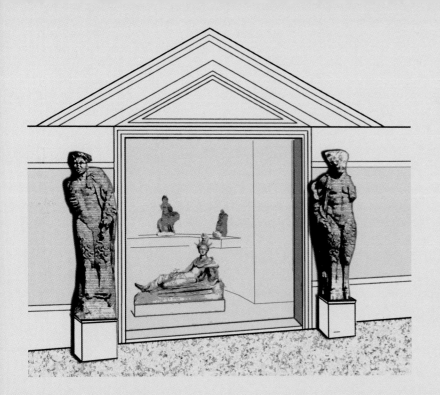

Shrine of Attis (figs. 30 and 31). Two large Pans frame the entrance, each holding a panpipe and a shepherd's crook. Within is C. Cartilius Euplus' dedication of a life-size marble figure of Attis and seven small statuettes. One of these is a figure of the Roman goddess Venus Genetrix. As often happens in Roman religion, devotees combine the worship of gods or goddesses in a process called syncretism. Because Venus is associated with Troy, an eastern city, devotees associate her with Cybele, the major goddess of the East. Although found out of place, a small chest crowned by a rooster and dedicated by M. Modius Maximus, high priest of Cybele, *archigallus coloniae Ostiensis,* probably fit in one of the niches. The rooster, *gallus* in Latin, is a pun on the title *archigallus,* or "head rooster."

II

WORK

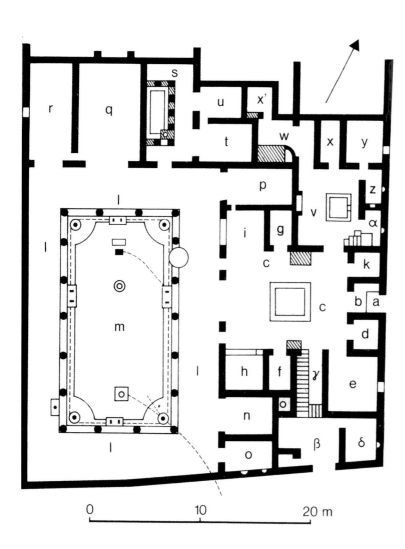

32 House of the Vettii, Pompeii. Plan

Restitutus Receives His Clients

"Except for the Emperor Vespasian, everybody is somebody's client," Aulus Vettius Restitutus thinks as he completes his sacrifice in the Lararium, for it is now time to receive his own clients. The daily ritual of the *salutatio* means that Restitutus—or his brother Conviva—has to open the house each morning to receive their clients—the people who run their various enterprises or are somehow dependent on them. When he was a slave running the wool-treating shop of his master Aulus Vettius *Faustus*, he had to wait in line every morning with all of his master's clients—some of them slaves, some freedmen, some freeborn workers. Now and again it would be a prominent Pompeian gentleman who came calling—usually just before the civic elections.

Restitutus leaves the slaves' atrium and makes his way through the great formal atrium to the large reception hall at the north end of the peristyle, room *q* (fig. 32). When planning their house, the brothers had decided to eliminate the traditional room for receiving clients, the *tablinum*. What they lost was the opportunity to stand in the tablinum and see each client enter from the street. What they gained through this arrangement was a much larger atrium —all the better to impress. In the mornings, it is a place for business transactions; in the evenings, it becomes one of the most elegant dining spaces in Pompeii.

In a moment of inspired whimsy, Restitutus and Conviva commissioned the picture-painter *Fidelis* to decorate the long, narrow frieze that runs around the lower part of the walls with scenes of work. After all, in the mornings this room sees a stream of clients who run various businesses for the wealthy freedmen, so why not? To their delight, Fidelis produced a frieze with diminutive cupids and psyches at work in practically all the industries common in Pompeii: garland making, perfume manufacture, goldsmithing, cloth-treating, bread-making, winemaking, and more (see CD-ROM).

The first client to arrive is *Marcus Holconius Asiaticus*, who bought the brothers' *fullonica* (cloth-treating plant) near the Forum. Asiaticus is an up-and-coming businessman, a former slave like Restitutus, who had the fortune to be owned by Marcus Holconius Rufus, son of one of the richest decurions in Pompeii. Asiaticus is here to tell Restitutus that he has completed remodeling and has expanded his business upward, as it were. The fullonica, installed in an old house with a traditional peristyle, had outgrown its space, and Asiaticus has created a huge second-story drying area by making a deck where the peristyle roof had been, replacing the elegant columns of the peristyle with heavy brick piers to support the weight of the drying racks. Restitutus

is pleased with this news, since he lent Asiaticus a thousand sesterces for these renovations; improved profits will feed directly back into Restitutus' pocket—with interest.

The next visitor is Restitutus' distinguished friend and neighbor, Lucius Caecilius Jucundus—a money man. He is freeborn but the son of a former slave, and he carries on the same businesses as his father: banking, auctioning, and collecting taxes—work that, no matter how lucrative, an upper-class citizen would avoid like the plague. In fact, some auctioneers who sell slaves (as Jucundus does) are blacklisted by the censors with the mark of infamy, just like prostitutes, actors, and gladiators.

But Jucundus is a valuable friend and political ally, and at least as rich as Restitutus and Conviva. Today, he simply needs Restitutus' signature as a witness to a land sale. He produces a wax tablet with the details and Restitutus signs it without even reading it.

His next caller, *Manius,* is the grandson of the famous Eumachia, priestess of Venus during the reign of Augustus (27 B.C.–A.D. 14). Eumachia had used her fortune to construct the most impressive building on the Forum, and now, seventeen years after the earthquake of 62 that brought poor Pompeii to its knees, Eumachia's building is still not restored.

A Banker's Record Books. In 1875, the archaeologist Antonio Sogliano excavated the house of L. Caecilius Jucundus, finding 154 wax tablets recording sums that he paid to persons for whom he had sold land, animals, and slaves between A.D. 52 and 60. Sogliano also found a bronze herm portrait in the atrium inscribed "From Felix to our patron Lucius," which is discussed in chapter VIII (see below and fig. 112).

33 BELOW House of L. Caecilius
Jucundus, Pompeii. Drawing of the
marble panels from the Lararium,
showing the effects of the earthquake
of A.D. 62 on Pompeii's Forum

34 OPPOSITE Forum, Pompeii. Drawing
of the portrait statue of Eumachia
in its original location in the Building
of Eumachia

For Manius, a wealthy decurion, it is a matter of family prestige that has spurred him to ask for the help of the Vettii brothers. After all, the inscription placed there by his grandmother glorified his father and grandfather. It is a disgrace to see it broken, parts of it lying on the ground. Miraculously, Eumachia's statue, dedicated by her freedmen, still stands at the back of the big building, unscathed by the earthquake.

For Restitutus and Conviva, investing in the rebuilding of Eumachia's building is an attractive proposition. Not only do they own a construction company, but many of their business interests center on Pompeii's wool industry. In fact, this is what the Vettii brothers and Eumachia's family have in common: The big building on the Forum serves as the largest emporium for buying and selling wool products—raw wool from the hinterlands as well as finished wool products. Although, as decurions, Eumachia's descendants

would never openly admit that they sully their hands with commerce, they have freedmen like the Vettii brothers and a great many slaves running a variety of businesses for them. Like all members of their class, they pretend that all their wealth is inherited—or that it comes from their landholdings—and delegate the day-to-day running of those businesses to enterprising slaves and freedmen.

Money is always a concern for men like Manius. For one thing, all his civic patronage— paying for gladiatorial games, for upkeep of buildings like his grandmother's emporium, and for bread and oil doles—costs him money. For another, no one of his class would ever directly receive pay for serving in the Senate, being a Consul (*duumvir*), or holding any of the public priesthoods. You buy prestige just as you buy votes. All that matters is increasing the glory of your clan.

▶ **The Earthquake of A.D. 62.**
A dramatic record of the earthquake that devastated Pompeii (an unheeded warning that Vesuvius was destined to erupt) comes from the Lararium in the house of Lucius Caecilius Jucundus (fig. 33).

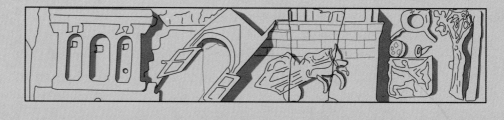

Asiaticus's Fullonica

As Asiaticus makes his way to his fullonica,
he wonders how his workers will react
to the centerpiece of the renovations
that Restitutus' loan has paid for. Today
they will see the new fountain that their
master has installed in the courtyard.
Several weeks ago Asiaticus hired a good
painter, *Spurius Italicus*, to decorate the
fountain, but in addition to the images
of his favorite deities and a propitious
serpent, Asiaticus insisted on celebrating
his workers at their jobs. So Spurius
made sketches of the women who work
the front of the shop. He spent some
time with his sketchbook at the treading
vats, and promised to capture the like-
nesses of each of Asiaticus's cloth treaders:
Gamus, *Pamphilus*, *Phoebus*, and his
favorite, *Eros*. Spurius sketched the big
Antiochene cloth bleacher, *Draco*, carrying his bleaching cage and a bucket of
sulfur. He even visited the new big racks
above the courtyard, where workers hang
cloth to dry. He sketched them combing
the wool and even made a sketch of the
big cloth press. Now it is time to unveil
his creation.

Eutyche and *Fortunata* emerge from
their quarters in back of the peristyle
to be the first to see the new fountain.

35 BELOW Fullonica, Pompeii.
Plan showing location of pier

36 RIGHT Fullonica, Pompeii.
Pier painted with wool-treating
scenes, south and east sides

37 OPPOSITE Fullonica, Pompeii.
Pier painted with wool-treating
scenes, east and north sides

◀ ▶ **An Important Pompeian Industry.**
There were many wool-treating
installations or fulleries *(fullonicae)*
in Pompeii. From the largest (which
I assign to the fictional Asiaticus)
comes a big painted pier outlined in
red (fig. 35), discovered in 1825 and
removed to the Naples Museum (figs.
36 and 37). A fullery provided two
services: finishing newly woven cloth
and cleaning soiled cloth. Although
one can use wool cloth immediately
after weaving, the processes collec-
tively called fulling are needed to
clean it further, shrink it (making it
thicker and fuller), soften it, bleach it
white, and give it a nap if desired.
Because the Romans had no soap to
cut the greasy lanolin on wool, the
first step was to wash the cloth in
warm water with a grease cutter such
as soapwort root, natron, potash, or
urine (both animal and human). The
next step was to rub in fuller's earth,
an adsorbent, clayey substance. After
washing the cloth again and beating
it, the fullers hung it to dry. Once dry,
it was combed with various kinds of
combs and then bleached with sulfur.
At this point the fullers rubbed the
cloth with fuller's earth again,
brushed it, and pressed it using a
large mechanical press (rather than
heated irons). Fulleries were not only
smelly, they also required a lot of
water and space for drying cloth. City
regulations forbade drying racks on
sidewalks, which forced owners like
Asiaticus to build upper-story drying
terraces supported by hefty piers.

38 ABOVE Fullonica, Pompeii. Decorative scheme of fountain, walls, and piers in the southeast part of the peristyle, seen from the southwest

39 OPPOSITE Carpentry shop, Pompeii. Carpenters' procession

Asiaticus has just entered the front of the shop and turned on the valve; the two piers begin to spurt water into the round basin between them (fig. 38). Rounding the corner, they see images of themselves. There on the top front is Fortunata, seated on a stool, about to take the darning needle from her little girl as she contemplates how to mend a piece. She doesn't mind the fact that the artist has made her and the little girl much smaller than the wool comber and Draco with his bleaching cage, which is made out of cane. After all, these men do the really tough work. Fortunata particularly appreciates the owl perched on top of the bleaching cage: Minerva's bird is both a symbol of the

goddess and a visual prayer that she will protect all the wool workers and allow them to prosper.

The two women take in the scene below with some relish, because here the artist has depicted their favorites—the sturdy men who work the treading vats in back of the shop. They are not surprised that the artist has made Eros so much bigger than his coworkers. Not only is he much better looking than the other three, it's clear that their owner, Asiaticus, wants to free him, adopt him, and turn the fullery over to him. But the disparity in scale *is* a bit laughable, making the other workers look like children. Eutyche suppresses a giggle as Pamphilus rounds the corner, for his image is the funniest of the four, looking for all the world like a prematurely bald schoolchild treading away with determination in the second vat from the right.

The right side of the pier holds a pleasant surprise for Fortunata, for it's clear that Spurius has gone out of his way to flatter her. He's shown her wearing her best gold chiton and a lovely (but impractical) blue mantle draped over her right arm as she accepts a cloth drop-off from a handsome slave in a blue tunic. And off to the right sits Artemesia, smartly decked out as well, carefully cleaning a wool comb.

As the workers gather around Asiaticus, who sacrifices some cakes and fruits on a portable altar set up at the fountain for the occasion, they feel quite special. Their master, a former slave who made his way up and bought his freedom, owns them, but he has flattered them and given them an incentive to save up their weekly allowance to purchase their freedom just as he did. Somehow, seeing themselves at work in such nice portraits and with such accurate depictions of their jobs dignifies their toil and gives them hope for the future.

◀ **The Carpenters' Procession.** This image of the carpenters carrying a bier in the form of a little temple came from the front of a woodworking shop at Pompeii (fig. 39). The men wear tunics cinched up at the waist and lean on canes to help support the weight. Their patron deities occupy either end of the bier. All that remains of the image of Minerva on the left is her shield, but the figure of the master craftsman, Daedalus, standing over the body of his nephew, Perdix, still occupies the right end of the display. In between, we see carpenters at work. One man, next to Minerva's shield, is planing a board. To the right, two men saw a big plank. The shop's facade also included another image of Daedalus, this time presenting his famous wooden cow to Pasiphae (see CD-ROM), along with images of Mercury and Fortune, but these, left in place, have been destroyed by the elements.

Verecundus and Lollia's Clothing Shop on Main Street

M. Vecilius Verecundus and his wife *Lollia* are opening up their big clothing shop on Pompeii's main street. In earlier years, they had run various cloth-making and cloth-treating plants, like Asiaticus. But now they leave the hard labor to others, many of them slaves, or freedmen clients like Asiaticus, and sell finished goods in their well-stocked shop—cloth and clothing of every sort, from fine Egyptian linen tunics embroidered in gold to hooded raincoats made of heavy felt. Some years earlier, Verecundus employed the services of Spurius Italicus to decorate the facade of their new shop. It turned out to be a complicated business, but in the end, the expense was worth the trouble. The problem was deciding whether to do the traditional thing and feature the deities who protected the shop, or to show the passersby what Verecundus and Lollia were selling. Eventually they settled on a compromise, giving the gods pride of place—for good fortune dictated that—but also showing both Verecundus and Lollia at work. To emphasize the wide range of goods for sale, they decided to highlight two very different kinds of manufacture with a scene of wool-combing and one of felt-making. It is an eclectic mix but it draws curious customers into the shop.

Arguably, the biggest draw is the big, beautiful image of Pompeii's patron deity, Venus Pompeiana, in her elephant-drawn chariot, flanked by the goddess Fortuna on the left and the genius of Verecundus on the right (fig. 40). It is the perfect merging of piety and business. Just as Venus protects the colony of Pompeii, so Fortuna, with her rudder to steer things right and her cornucopia to pour out blessings, will make the couple's business prosper. And to emphasize who is in charge of the business end of things, Verecundus' genius stands, head veiled in sacrifice, right over the image of the real Verecundus in the little frieze below.

Verecundus particularly likes the portrait Spurius painted of him—not a stodgy formal portrait but the very image of a shopkeeper at work, holding up a fine brown cloth decorated with purple stripes. So that everyone may know who he is, there is his name in clear letters below: VERECUNDUS.

Lollia is glad that she has her own space, on the narrower pier to the left of the doorway, for it gave Spurius free rein to re-create her favorite part of the shop (fig. 41). And there she is at the center of it all, sitting behind a high table, dressed in her favorite blue hooded

40 OPPOSITE Shop of Verecundus, Pompeii. Pier between doorways 7 and 5. Above: Venus Pompeiana. Below: Clothworkers with Verecundus at right

41 RIGHT Shop of Verecundus, Pompeii. Left pier of doorway 7. Sales scene with woman and customer

mantle with a shoe in either hand, for one of the shop's specialties is sturdy waterproof shoes made of felt. To display more of the wares, Spurius painted a second table projecting out into the foreground with a glass vase, four shoes, and red and yellow bundles of cloth on either side. But the nicest touch is that Spurius put a customer in the scene, sitting on a fine wooden bench and modeling one of their special blue hooded mantles as he turns and gestures toward Lollia.

Of course, Lollia's picture is smaller than that of Mercury (fig. 42). One wouldn't want to slight the god of commerce. Spurius created a magnificent and dignified image—not one of those vulgar phallic Mercuries you saw in common wineshops. He placed the god on the porch of a fine temple, fully clothed, his wand *(caduceus)* in one hand and his money bag *(marsupium)* in the other. The wings on his hat and on his shoes promise speed in returning profits to the couple's shop.

Although Lollia's friends and customers often comment on Spurius's fine portrayal of her sales counter, it is the artist's depiction of the felt makers that makes them stop and look. Few Pompeians have

ventured into the hot and smelly interior of a felt-making establishment, so people speculate about what the four sturdy men—scantily clad in short kilts—are doing as they seem to be kneading long white strands on twin teardrop-shaped basins resting on sawhorses (fig. 43). They are felting—pressing wool and animal hairs together into a compact, consistent mass by working hot glue into the fibers. The basins feed the cooling glue back into the boiler at the center to be reheated by the little log fire. The felt sheds water, making it perfect for hats, boots, slippers, and raincoats; soldiers even use it for breastplates and tents.

To balance out this arresting scene of heavy industry, Spurius filled out the rest of the frieze with three nearly identical images of wool combers, each seated before a low combing table fitted with two tall combs, one behind the other. Their job is to ready the raw wool for spinning by pulling it through the combs to remove knots and residue. Although Spurius could have pictured other stages of the wool-treating and weaving industry, the three wool combers fit nicely into the limited space and show what the couple's shop is about.

42 OPPOSITE Shop of Verecundus, Pompeii. Left pier of doorway 7, Mercury in His Temple

43 ABOVE Shop of Verecundus, Pompeii. Right pier of doorway 7. Detail, feltmakers

A Middleman at the Top:
P. Aufidius Fortis

A.D. 160

44 **44** Forum of the Corporations, Ostia. Axonometric drawing showing the theater, temple, and offices (*stationes*) of the guilds

It's a hot July morning, and Publius Aufidius Fortis has a busy day ahead. Last evening, three of his huge grain ships came into Trajan's harbor at Portus, and he must get their cargo offloaded. The big ships—each holding a thousand tons—can't take the wheat directly to Rome and unload there, because the Tiber is too swift and winding. He must hire smaller boats to unload the cargo in the harbor and transport it to his big warehouse in Ostia for safekeeping while he arranges for its final sale and transportation to Rome. Just yesterday, he called on his friend Publius Peregrinus, Senator and prefect of supplies for Rome, letting him know that this huge shipment is on its way and hinting at the price he wanted.

Feeding a city of over a million people—most of them dependent on doles of wheat, oil, and money—is a huge enterprise, and Fortis realizes enormous profits from this sometimes risky business. This time his ships made it, thanks to calm weather and an able crew. Now to get the grain to Rome without spoilage, fire, or theft.

No one in Ostia is better able to do so than Fortis. The grain trade has been his lifelong career; he is the preeminent grain merchant in Ostia, and lifelong member of the grain merchant's guild.

His family has ties with Hippo Regius in Africa, one of the main grain-shipping ports of North Africa. He has traveled there frequently throughout his career to arrange the purchase and shipment of wheat, and eventually Hippo Regius made him a member of its city council. He is no less important in Ostia, where he is an elected duumvir and now enjoys the honor of being patron of the city. And, recently, the grain measurers named him patron of their guild.

Fortis decides to cut short the reception of his clients this morning, except for two—his former slaves Publius Aufidius Faustianus and Publius Aufidius Epictetus. Fortis has trained them carefully in the wheat trade, making sure that they also hold offices in the grain merchants' guild. He has helped them start their own more modest grain-trading businesses, and they're the right people to make sure his cargo gets safely offloaded and stored. They can also negotiate the best prices from the river boat companies to get the grain from his warehouses to Rome. It's agreed: Faustianus and Epictetus will immediately go over to the Forum of the Corporations and arrange the offloading and warehousing of Fortis' 3,000 tons of African wheat.

The Forum of the Corporations

Like their former master, Faustianus and Epictetus rely on various guilds to provide the services they need, so it's time to head to the Forum of the Corporations, where most of the guilds (*collegia* or *corpora*) they need to deal with have their little offices (fig. 44). When Emperor Augustus built Ostia's theater 150 years ago, he provided the usual porticus to shelter theatergoers when it rained. But when Emperor Hadrian remodeled the porticus, he doubled its width by adding a colonnade. Now the various guilds and businesses have small offices there that one can easily find by reading the mosaic signboards set into the pavements of the portico.

Faustianus and Epictetus enter the porticus through a gateway by the back of the theater. They pass by the offices of the tanners of Ostia and Portus, the rope sellers (although they will need new tow ropes when they begin to send the small boats upriver next week), and the timber shippers, and arrive at the first of several offices with the insignia of the grain-measurers in front. As officeholders in the guild of grain measurers, Faustianus and Epictetus get a rousing welcome. All the representatives on duty emerge from their offices at once, knowing that Fortis' big ships have arrived and there will be plenty of work for the grain measurers.

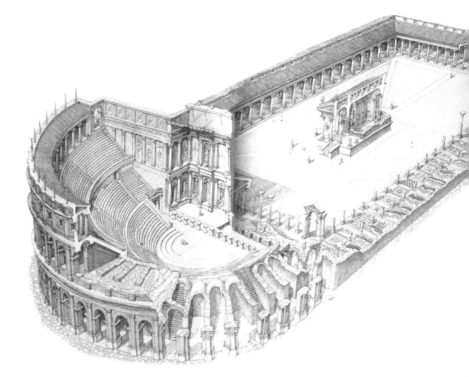

The grain measurers are essential at every step: not only to measure the grain, but to sack it and haul it off the big grain ships moored in Trajan's harbor at Portus; to oversee its safe transport and deposit in Fortis' warehouses at Ostia; and to get it safely loaded on the small boats that haul the grain up the Tiber to Rome, where other grain measurers take over. Faustianus and Epictetus discuss the size of the operation and the number of measurers needed with the guild's representatives. Then they move down the row of offices to speak with the representatives running the small harbor boats that routinely carry goods from the big merchantmen to the docks at Portus or to warehouses at Ostia, and contract for a fleet to begin work this evening.

Now that prices and schedules are agreed upon, the representatives with whom Faustianus and Epictetus had spoken send messengers—one to the grain measurers' guild hall, several others to Portus, to round up the necessary workers. Faustianus takes his leave of Epictetus and decides to take a leisurely walk to the Hall of the Grain Measurers. It's still not too late to stop by his favorite grocer's shop, owned by his old friend *Primigenia*, to order delicacies for this evening's feast. Epictetus hastens to his home, for he has family matters on his mind. His daughter Secunda may make him a grandfather this evening—if not sooner.

26

45 BELOW Forum of the Corporations,
Ostia. Grain Measurer with Bushel
Measure and Leveling Stick

46 OPPOSITE Forum of the Corporations,
Ostia. *Stationes* 26, 27, and 28, Nile River
with Animals

▲ **Offices of the Grain Measurers.**
The grain measurers have the
greatest number of offices in the
Forum of the Corporations, to judge
from the surviving mosaics, each
showing their essential emblem:
the bushel measure (fig. 45).

▶ **Cargoes.** Several of the mosaics
of the *stationes* in the Forum of
the Corporations show more exotic
cargoes than the usual wheat,
oil, and wine. The fine Nile River

mosaic, originally making up
three *stationes* (26, 27, and 28),
shows three wild animals on one
of its sides: an elephant, a deer,
and a wild boar (fig. 46). Like
statio 14, with the image of an
elephant and the inscription
stat(io) Sabrantensium (representing the city of Sabratha in North
Africa), this *statio* probably
specialized in the importation
of exotic beasts for display and
hunt in Rome's Colosseum.

27 28

▼ **Unloading a Grain Ship.** Grain measurers load the *Isis Giminiana* with a cargo of grain (fig. 47). Standing on the cabin in the stern is Farnaces, the ship's master, at the dual rudder. In the middle of the boat the grain measurer Arascanius checks the pouring of the wheat from a sack into the measure. To his right is a man holding a counter like the one in the mosaic from the Hall of the Grain Measurers. To the far right a man reclines, flanked by a second measurer inscribed with the word *feci:* "I have done my work." There is no sign of sails; the mast is probably for a towing rope.

◀ ▶ **The Grain Measurers' Guild Hall.** Ostia's grain measurers had at least one large guild hall, located on the road that led down to the port and warehouses at the mouth of the Tiber (figs. 48 and 49). The boy with a device that looks like a down-turned branch is using a simple counting instrument—like the man aboard the *Isis Giminiana.* It is a cord onto which he adds a wooden stick for each unit that the measurers handle. The presence of a boy in this mosaic underscores the Romans' ample use of child labor—whether slave or freeborn. The inscription, although damaged at the time of discovery, probably says "Six workers of the Agilianus Warehouse here."

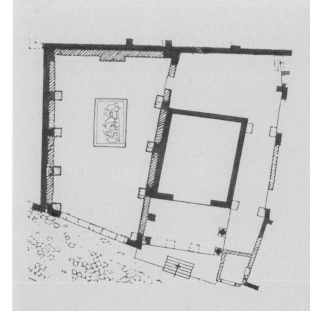

▼ **A Woman's Food Store.** Most representations of working women show them engaged in sales or service occupations, and this relief from a shop at Ostia is no exception (fig. 50). What is exceptional is the artist's keen portrayal of the owner's lively personality (I have called her *Primigenia*). A woman to the right of center stands behind a counter made up of three cages. She engages a diminutive man as she hands him some sort of round vegetable or fruit with her right hand while grasping another with her left. We see just the head and shoulders of another person (her assistant?) behind the counter. On top of the middle crate are three stacked baskets; the artist has represented their contents by depicting a snail at the top left of the stack. The saleswoman's pet monkeys, put there as curiosities to attract customers, turn toward each other in three-quarter view, the one on the left scratching its head. Beaks of fowl—probably chickens—peck at grain in the gutter at the base of two of the crates, while two hares stick their heads out of the crate on the right. The man standing to the left and gesturing broadly toward the dead hare could be a coproprietor, or he could be a customer. The one unambiguous proprietor is the woman, a point the artist reinforced by giving her an assistant who looks out over her right arm.

Women at Work

Primigenia has a distinct advantage over Fortunata and Eutyche, who got to see themselves in the fountain painting of their fullonica every day, or even Lollia, who took center stage in the painting on the facade of her clothing shop. She is neither a slave like the fullonica workers nor merely the owner's wife, like Lollia. Primigenia owns her own grocery store. Although born a slave in the house of her mistress, *Claudia Quinta*, Primigenia's winning personality and sharp business sense soon had her running several of Quinta's enterprises, including the store she now owns. She bought her freedom and her small establishment.

Every morning, Primigenia rises early enough to meet the local farmers at one of the markets set up outside the city gates to choose fresh produce, poultry, hares—and sometimes snails—to stock her shop. Her own right-hand man is a slave, *Felix*, who makes up in brawn what he lacks in brains. Primigenia handles the accounts, Felix the hauling and delivery. Once the shop began prospering, Primigenia called in the sculptor *Ephesios* to carve an elegant sign to advertise what she sells—and incidentally to immortalize herself, her pet monkeys, and Felix.

Isola Sacra. Terracotta relief from tomb
100, of the doctor, M. Ulpius Amerimnus,
and the midwife, Scribonia Attice. A woman
is seated on a birthing chair

It's evening of that same day, and Scribonia Attice is in a hurry. She has just gotten word that a patient's water has broken. She is Secunda, the younger daughter of Publius Aufidius Epictetus, the grain merchant. Scribonia is Ostia's best midwife (*obstetrix*). Like her husband, Marcus Ulpius Amerimnus, she is Greek and studied medicine in Ephesus with the great Soranus. Unlike many doctors, both Scribonia and her husband are freeborn citizens. Most doctors, talented and not-so-talented, are slaves trained in Greece and bought by wealthy Romans to attend to their health, or else they are former military surgeons.

It was Soranus' gynecological treatises, the *Gynaecia*, the best works on women's medicine, that inspired Scribonia to specialize in midwifery. There are far too many poorly trained midwives, who lack the knowledge that could save the lives of mother and child. And far too few know the techniques and remedies that Soranus recommends.

Scribonia has already examined Secunda several times and is reasonably sure of an easy delivery—even though this is her first child. Following Soranus' prescriptions, Scribonia has asked the family to prepare a quiet room in their house for the delivery, furnished with two beds—a firm one that Secunda can stretch out on before the birth, and another, softer one to rest on afterward. Most important of all is the birthing chair with its semicircular opening in the seat and two strong grips at the sides. Scribonia has made sure all the necessaries will be provided: hot compresses, olive oil, soft sponges, textiles, and a pillow on which to place the baby immediately after birth. Three experienced women will assist. Scribonia has chosen Secunda's childhood nanny, another trusted family slave, and her own assistant, *Myrina*. These three will help calm Secunda and then hold her still during her labor in the birthing chair.

Scribonia arrives at the house of Secunda and her husband, Lucius Caecilius Aprilis, a grain trader from Carthage. Within an hour or so it is time for Scribonia to take her place beneath Secunda on a low stool, calmly instructing her while the three assistants restrain her. When the right time comes, Scribonia oils her hands with hot olive oil and introduces a finger of her left hand to help dilate the opening. As the contractions become more violent and painful, Scribonia admonishes Secunda to keep her breathing in her chest and not to scream, but rather to follow and encourage the contractions when they come. At the moment of maximum dilation, Scribonia deftly pulls the baby toward her, while the assistants on either side push gently on Secunda's belly from top to bottom. She places a healthy, yelling baby boy on the big, cloth-covered pillow.

III

THE SPOILS OF WAR

A Soldier's Life Immortalized

A.D. 113

The news of the hour is that the great
column in the Forum of Trajan is
complete. *Theodorus Trajanus* is eager
to see the column, for it depicts the
two campaigns of the war against the
Dacians that occupied so much of his life
and won him Roman citizenship. As a
young man of Greek blood, he realized that
he could make his fortune as an auxiliary
in the Roman army. He learned all the
skills of a Roman soldier: how to march,
how to build bridges, roads, and fortifications, how to manage food supplies,
how to honor the gods, and how to fight.
Being part of such a disciplined and
well-organized fighting force appealed
to him. Toward the end of the second
campaign, the Emperor rewarded
Theodorus' cohort for their bravery,
granting citizenship to all the auxiliaries,
along with gifts of money and booty. This
is how Theodorus was able to make his
way to Rome after the destruction of
Sarmezegetusa, the Dacian capital. It was
an impressive homeward journey, the

52 FOLLOWING PAGES
View of the Column of Trajan
between the libraries, basilica,
and temple, Rome. Digital
reconstruction

53 OPPOSITE Forum of Trajan,
Basilica Ulpia, and Column of
Trajan from the south, Rome.
Digital reconstruction

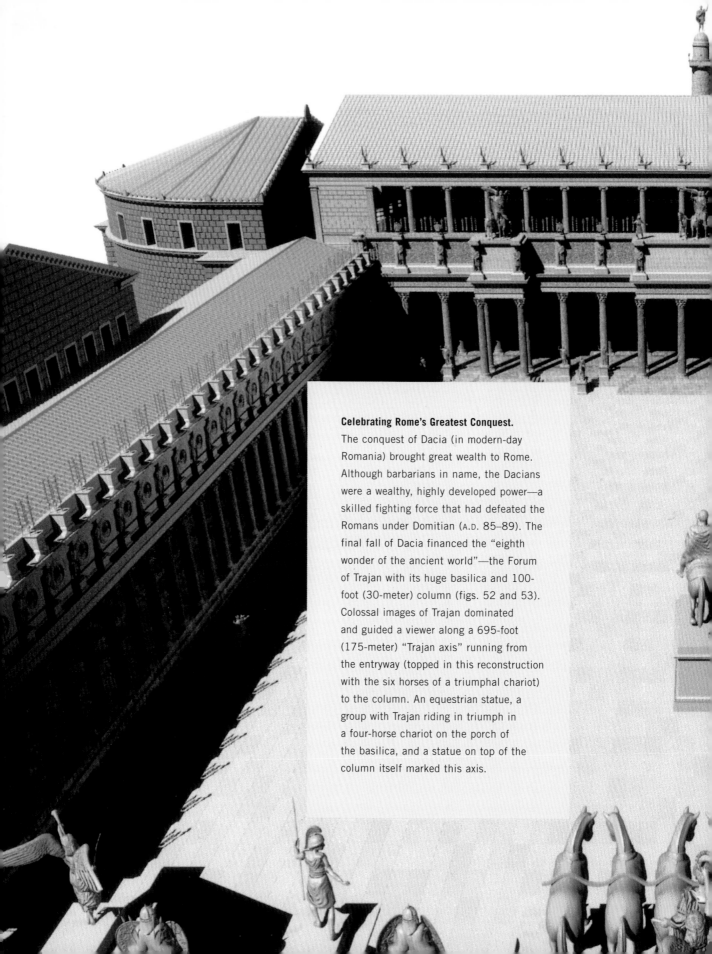

Celebrating Rome's Greatest Conquest.
The conquest of Dacia (in modern-day Romania) brought great wealth to Rome. Although barbarians in name, the Dacians were a wealthy, highly developed power—a skilled fighting force that had defeated the Romans under Domitian (A.D. 85–89). The final fall of Dacia financed the "eighth wonder of the ancient world"—the Forum of Trajan with its huge basilica and 100-foot (30-meter) column (figs. 52 and 53). Colossal images of Trajan dominated and guided a viewer along a 695-foot (175-meter) "Trajan axis" running from the entryway (topped in this reconstruction with the six horses of a triumphal chariot) to the column. An equestrian statue, a group with Trajan riding in triumph in a four-horse chariot on the porch of the basilica, and a statue on top of the column itself marked this axis.

54 BELOW Forum of Trajan, Rome.
Order of the east colonnade

55 OPPOSITE Column of Trajan,
Rome. Dedicated A.D. 113

victorious Romans carting the booty: silver, gold, and some 50,000 Dacian slaves.

Shortly after his arrival in Rome, Theodorus married the lovely *Salonina*, a former slave born in the home of her mistress, the wealthy Junia Calvina. They began a family, and today their six-year-old son, *Gnaeus Ulpius*, and four-year-old daughter, *Lucilla*, accompany them to see this great new wonder celebrating the war. Little Gnaeus has been boasting to his playmates about their outing today, and that there are pictures of the war his daddy helped the Emperor win.

The little family joins the throngs entering the new Forum under a huge triumphal arch. There's a shrine honoring Trajan, and images of the Emperor everywhere. As they begin to take in the enormous space, inspecting the huge colonnades that define it, Theodorus notices the names of legions and cohorts that he fought with inscribed high above statues of Dacians at least eight feet (2.5 meters) tall (fig. 54). He reads them aloud, and then with a thrill finds his own cohort, the first Lightning Cohort, with the wonderful letters *"c. R."* after it, proclaiming to everyone that Trajan had awarded citizenship to the entire cohort (about 500 men) for bravery in battle. In all, they count at least seventy-six units of auxiliary soldiers, both cavalry and infantry among the inscriptions—but only seventeen have the title of "Roman citizens" (*civium Romanorum*) after their unit's name.

They make their way slowly, taking in the rich colored marbles, the portraits framed by shields, and the names of the other victorious legions and cohorts. Everywhere the phrase *ex manubiis* reminds them that it was the spoils of the Dacian war that paid for all this magnificence.

Before looking at the column itself, Theodorus guides his family to the south porticus, where he's heard that paintings stretching along its length reproduce all the scenes that are carved on the Column. This will let them see all the details that are too far up on the Column. Trajan's book, *The History of the Dacian Wars*, must have guided the artists. There's the army crossing the Danube on the great bridge that Apollodorus of Damascus built, and there, too, the impressive scene that Theodorus and everyone else thought was the end of the war, when Decebalus, the Dacian leader, staged the submission to the Emperor and his army that ended the first campaign (A.D. 101–102). But Decebalus had other plans, and started hostilities again.

Little Gnaeus quickly figures out who the Emperor is, unmistakable in his gilded breastplate as he guides his soldiers through every detail of the war. There he is leading the troops over the Danube bridge, directing them as they cut trees and build fortifications, receiving delegations of barbarians, and above all preparing his troops for battle by

◀ **Organizing the Fighting Force.**
The secret to Rome's success in
building and maintaining so vast
an empire for such a long time was
the organization and management
of Roman military forces. The
images on the Column not only
celebrate the success of Trajan's
two campaigns in Dacia, they also
demonstrate—in some 150 scenes
with 2,500 figures—how and why
the Roman army won its wars (fig.
55). The Roman army in Trajan's
time consisted of about 350,000
men: several thousand praetorians
(the Emperor's elite guards),
140,000 regular soldiers (legionar-
ies), and about 200,000 auxiliaries.
The auxiliaries, recruited from
among former barbarians, did not
possess Roman citizenship. For
them, the prize to be won—in
addition to their meager pay—was
Roman citizenship. The artist represents all the ranks, spelling out
the hierarchies within the Roman
chain of command. Trajan is ever-
present, commanding all ranks,
from his top advisers all the way
down to the most exotic and un-
Roman barbarian troops in Rome's
employ. Trajan oversees every detail
of the campaigns: He marches with
the troops, supervises the building
of garrisons, sacrifices to the gods,
rouses his troops to fight, commands the battles, and receives
barbarian delegations (fig. 56).
Just like the Roman state, the
Roman army depended on clear,
top-down organization.

56 BELOW Column of Trajan,
Rome. Trajan addresses his
troops before battle

57 OPPOSITE Column of Trajan,
Rome. Scenes 42–45, the *dona
militaria*

carefully carrying out the sacrifices to
the gods and then addressing the troops.
Theodorus remembers those speeches
quite well and the bravery they inspired.
Then there are the battle scenes, filled
with details that make clear distinctions
between the fighting men: from Trajan
himself to the wildest-looking of the
auxiliaries fighting with their native
weapons. The distinctions among the
Dacians are clear, too. Their leaders
wear turbans, while the fighting men
have shaggy hair and beards. And
marked out as clearly as Trajan is his
great adversary, Decebalus.

Now it's time to see the Column itself.
They make their way up the steps of the
huge Basilica, named the Ulpia after
Trajan's family. Salonina reminds her son
that his second name, Ulpius, is in honor
of Trajan. From the cavernous basilica
(said to be the largest covered space in
the world) they make their way to the
plaza at the back, where the Column rises
up between the two libraries. The sculptors have covered the huge base with
images of Dacian weapons and standards;
little Lucilla is fascinated by the Dacians'
eerie standards in the form of long,
snakelike creatures floating overhead.

Lots of neck-craning and squinting ensue as Theodorus and his family try to follow the windings to the top—an impossible task, they soon realize. But they also realize that the sculptors worked out another way to get the main story. They repeat a pattern using stock scenes: the Romans march, make camp, receive Dacian ambassadors and then prepare for battle. Every battle begins with a solemn sacrifice led by Trajan, then his address to the assembled troops. These patterns they can make out, and they can also spot the figure of Victory about halfway up. She writes on a shield—an image of a short-lived victory—right after the scene of the Dacians surrendering after the first campaign.

Gnaeus is the first to start an amusing game. He calls it "find the Emperor," and Lucilla invents another: "find the Decebalus." They all realize that it is not hard to pick out either Trajan or Decebalus, as long as you let your eyes go up and down instead of trying to follow the windings that go from left to right. Theodorus considers his good fortune even while remembering the long and dangerous path that led to this happy moment.

► **Rewards for Bravery.** Outstanding auxiliaries could receive rewards of money—or even citizenship—for outstanding bravery in battle (fig. 57). In this scene, Trajan sits on a portable camp stool with his aides behind him while an auxiliary soldier (wearing a short leather jerkin, trousers, and a cape) bends to kiss his hand. Another auxiliary walks away with a sack containing money or booty on his shoulder, while below, two auxiliary soldiers kiss. The artist has positioned this scene between two images of the enemy. To the left, Dacian men— both the officials wearing turbans and the ordinary fighters with shaggy hair—stand within a fortified city; to the right, Dacian women torture naked and bound Roman soldiers with firebrands.

IV
SHOWS

Marcus Holconius Rufus
A.D. 10

It's a holiday for everyone in Pompeii—
even the slaves—and they have Marcus
Holconius Rufus to thank. The whole day
will be devoted to the theater, with comedy and tragedy set off by entertaining
mimes brought in from Naples; in the
evening, the most famous pantomime in
Rome, favorite of the Emperor Augustus
himself, will perform. Marcus Holconius
Rufus has paid for all of this. "My duty,"
he thinks, as he rises and puts on his best
toga. "My duty and my burden," he
almost says aloud, remembering just how
much it has cost—not just the day at the
theater, but also the renovations he and
his brother, Marcus Holconius Celer,
have paid for. Yet this is how a proper
decurion must and should act, spending
all he can to bring glory to his clan to make
the Holconii the first family of Pompeii.

As he makes his way to the theater,
surrounded by the official bodyguards
(*lictors*) who belong to his office as high
counselor of the city (*quinquennial
duumvir*), Rufus recalls the way the old
theater looked before the work began.
It was Roman in form but with rude
wooden bleachers, a paltry scene building

58 The Large Theater, Pompeii.
View from the top row of seats

(scaenae frons), and low tribunals. Worst
of all, it lacked the means to control the
crowd and channel people into their
proper seating areas. Sometimes mere
freedmen would pass through the lowest
row of seats reserved for decurions like
himself, and once he even saw a slave
sneaking down to the middle area reserved
for freeborn citizens and freedmen.

Rufus and Celer have transformed the
theater into a marble wonder—just like
the great Augustus, who said that he
found Rome a city of mud brick and left it
one of marble. Of course, it's on a much
more modest scale than anything in
Rome, but Augustus has noticed and

rewarded Rufus and the gens Holconia.
Four years ago, the Emperor made Rufus
a priest of Augustus so that he could wear
the official regalia at the inauguration of
the Ara Pacis, the Altar of Peace in Rome.

Rufus arrives at the theater (fig. 58).
He mounts the tribunal to the right just
as, in an inspired act of perfect timing,
his brother Celer mounts the tribunal
to the left. The crowd cheers. There's a
special surprise for Rufus. Several city
officials are unveiling a monument to him,
located just above one of the tiers of seats
reserved for the decurions. It's a bronze
curule chair, the kind of seat a magistrate
sits on—a fitting symbol of his office as

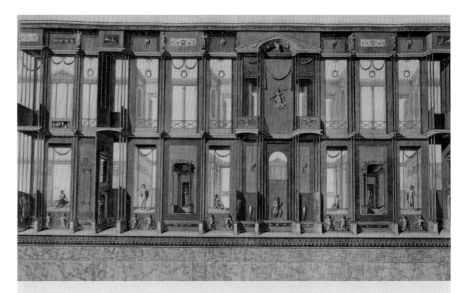

▲ ▶ **Recreating the *Scaenae Frons*.**
In Roman theaters, actors performed
in front of a stage building called
the *scaenae frons,* a high wall decorated with temple fronts that con-
tained statues. Stage scenery, when
available, fit in the back of the
shallow stage with the rest of the
scaenae frons visible above. The
statues in the *scaenae frons* often
represented the Emperor and his
family, along with the patrons of the
theater—constantly reminding the
public that the theater was a gift
from the powers-that-be. Artists
often represented versions of the
stage building in wall paintings of
the first century (fig. 59). Here we
see an artist's record of a wall from
the Emperor Nero's Golden House
(A.D. 64–68). The statues in the
niches seem more like living persons
than stone sculptures. A bit later,
this painting (opposite) from a bath
at Pompeii animates the statues and
makes them into athletes descending
stairways from their niches to the
stage podium (fig. 60).

chief city counselor. One of his lictors hands Rufus a scroll with the text of the inscription, which reads:

"Dedicated in accordance with a decree of the city council to Marcus Holconius Rufus the son of Marcus, five times duumvir with judiciary authority, twice quinquennial duumvir, military tribune by choice of the people, priest of Augustus, and patron of the colony." *M. Holconio M. F. Rufo, II.v.i.d. quinquiens, iter(um) quinq(uennali), trib(uno) mil(itum) a p(opolo), flamini Aug(usti), patr(ono) colo(niae), d(ecurionum) d(ecreto).*

The decurions could not have created a more gratifying monument to unveil at this moment, especially considering how much

money and effort Rufus has put into this project. With all this attention on him, Rufus is glad that he made sure his brother's role in renovating and improving the theater got recorded as well. There are two identical inscriptions placed over side entrances that read: "Marcus Holconius Rufus and Marcus Holconius Celer [built] the crypta, the tribunals, and the seating with their own money." *M(arcus) et M(arcus) Holconii Rufus et Celer cryptam tribunalia theatrum s(ua) p(ecunia).*

But there's more to come. Rufus and Celer have just engaged several sculptors to decorate the new *scaenae frons* with

statues of the Emperor, his wife Livia, and the most important family members represented on the Ara Pacis. He hopes that the decurions will insist on putting his statue (and perhaps Celer's) in the *scaenae frons* as well. Now everyone who comes to the theater will associate the gens Holconia with the Emperor and his family. It has taken a lot of money, but Marcus' status and that of the gens Holconia is assured for generations to come. His sons are now perfectly positioned to continue to bring glory to the gens: The Holconii will remain the first family of Pompeii.

Annia Lucilla

Annia Lucilla, Marcus' wife, leaves the house at about the same time as her husband, but because of Augustus' new law meant to bring order to the theater, she won't be sitting with him in his tribunal. Augustus has insisted that women take their place in the highest tier of the theater—with foreigners and slaves of all people! Not that it's a great sacrifice for Annia, since she is surrounded by the best women of Pompeii, and all of them by their handsomest slaves. And Rufus and Celer have built them a pleasant seating area—in marble, no less. Although it's a long way down to the stage, the seats are comfortable and the sound good. And today—thanks to her husband—there will be a full sun shade, supported on masts and stretched on rigging provided by the local Roman navy.

Although Annia is not much for tragedy (today they're offering a rewrite of Euripides' *Medea* by the Latin playwright Pacuvius), she is looking forward to a revival of Plautus' *Boll Weevil (Curculio)*. It is her favorite play, first performed almost 200 years ago, and still very, very funny. In those days, Plautus had to pretend that all his naughty characters were Greeks, so that he wouldn't make the scrapping aristocrats and their

Pairs of Fighting Gladiators. Nine pairs of gladiators appear in the relief, beginning on the right with a pair of equestrian gladiators who have just dismounted. The other eight pairs all show a *thrax,* or Thracian, fighting his traditional adversary, the *myrmillo* (fig. 61). The pair on either end looks inward to frame the action, and dynamic figures—standing and moving—alternate with static ones. Several figures turn their backs toward the viewer. The secondary, noncombatant figures, probably referees, appear in shallower relief.

scheming, disobedient children look like the Romans of his day. But everyone got the point anyway!

Annia arrives at her seat in the center of the uppermost tier, and looks down at all the men. She nods discreetly to Rufus and Celer in their twin tribunals when the crowd cheers them, and again, when they unveil the new bronze monument to her husband. She looks to the orchestra and the lowest tier of seating where the decurions sit—all wearing their togas with broad purple stripes—and tries to identify every one. Next tier up are the equestrians, wearing togas with narrow purple stripes. Annia knows some of these men as well; in fact, many of them report frequently to Rufus about how they're running the businesses in which he's invested. As for the next tier, of men wearing plain white wool togas, Annia hasn't a clue without the help of her slave, whose job it is to know the name of everyone who is someone. After all, among those citizen men there might be

a rich freedman worth knowing—maybe even one of *her* freedmen. After looking at all that bleached white wool, it's a relief to look around her own section. It's a riot of color—not to mention the fantastic variety of silks and linens. Annia carefully fixes her finely embroidered silk mantle and adjusts a lock of hair that's fallen free of her hairdo—a perfect replica of Empress Livia's.

Pylades

"Being a pantomime must be the hardest work in the Roman Empire," thinks Pylades, as he prepares for his special performance at Pompeii—of all places. "I have to carry the whole performance. I have to play every character—man, woman, and child. And I have to make it look like no work at all." Pylades has been watching the long festival fitfully throughout the day, knowing that no matter how well or badly the other actors

62 Monument of Storax, Chieti.
Pediment showing Storax presiding
over the games (before A.D. 40)

do, he's the one the crowd will judge with the greatest severity, for he is the pantomime of the moment, "By appointment to the court," one might say, since the Emperor himself has awarded him lavish gifts and honors. Even when he wins his freedom, Pylades will continue to endure the legal status of infamy—just like prostitutes, gladiators, and passive homosexuals. Officially, Pylades is something less than a citizen because he displays his body for the people's entertainment, just as prostitutes and gladiators do. What matter? His consummate command of his difficult art wins everyone over.

He thinks how much easier his work would be, had he been content to don the masks and costumes of tragedy and comedy, learn the playwrights' lines, and declaim with a voice loud enough to be heard by the women and slaves in the uppermost tier. But that was not enough. The high art of pantomime called him—in the guise of his Greek master *Erotis*. As a boy, he had watched his teacher mount the stage and take it over, changing personas without the help of masks. He could tell any tale—even the most complex—with facial expressions, dancelike movement, and song. One moment he was the tormented Pentheus, the next moment Pentheus' mother, Agave, a raving maenad.

In fact, this afternoon Pylades will pantomime the tragedy of Pentheus and Agave, who discover the power of Bacchus. It is a new work based on Euripides' timeless *Bacchae*, first performed in Athens 400 years ago. In the meantime, he watches the actors and musicians marching in—not for comedy or tragedy, but to perform the real audience-pleaser: the Adultery Mime. Pylades has nothing against popular theater, but it shouldn't be on the legitimate stage. Mimes belong in the street—or at best in simple festivals set up in the Forum or outside the city walls. But everyone loves the mime—and why shouldn't they? The troupe performing the Adultery Mime today is among the best. Pylades has seen them before. The beautiful *Phryne* plays the faithless wife, the handsome *Hyacinthus* her young lover. And today it's the incomparable *Gamus* who plays the cuckolded husband. Gamus has the stage business down pat. When he comes home unexpectedly and Hyacinthus must jump out of the bed and into a trunk to hide, Gamus plays with that trunk like a dog with a bone—first tapping it, then moving it, then kicking it—all the while

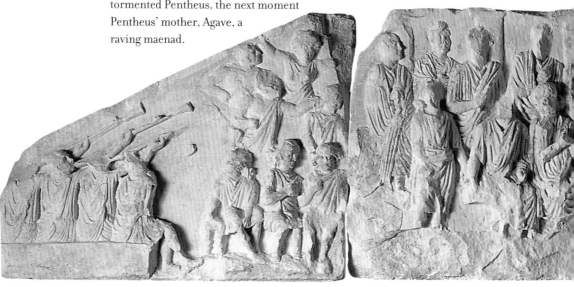

pretending he doesn't know Hyacinthus is in there. Of course, Phryne pretends that she can't find the key. When Gamus finally takes an axe to it and Phyrne extracts poor Hyacinthus from the trunk, the audience is in an uproar. Great fun—but not real theater.

Lusius Storax

In the little town of Teate Marrucinorum (modern Chieti, thirteen miles [twenty kilometers] inland from Pescara, on Italy's Adriatic coast), an event like today's games is news indeed; but the real news is that the person paying for this lavish day of games is a former slave well known to all: Gaius Lusius Storax, freedman of Gaius. No one could be happier than Storax's slave *Anicetus*, since in preparation for this happy event Storax has granted him freedom. Today, for the first time, Anicetus will wear the toga—with the cap of liberty—to let everyone know his good fortune.

Teate is a city with excellent defenses, built on the highest hill in the area, about twelve miles (eighteen kilometers) inland from the Adriatic sea. Now—thanks to the

gifts of the town's decurions and rich Augustales like Storax—it boasts an amphitheater. But before the games can begin, there are rites that must be attended to. Anicetus follows the throng to Teate's Forum, where Storax is about to perform a sacrifice at the temple of the Capitoline gods. Storax is giver of the games, a privilege he has paid for but a privilege nonetheless. Today he is the first among the first. The sacrifice is elaborate and lavish—there will be plenty of roast meat after the games. Since Storax is a former slave, it is only because the Emperor Augustus has made him an Augustalis that he is permitted to perform the sacrifice and give the games. In fact, Storax is surrounded by Augustales, the other five serving this year and the six who served last year. He is also surrounded by the lictors, the heralds, and, of course, the decurions. It is this group of august citizen males that now close ranks behind Storax. It is time for the great procession (*pompa*) to wind its way up to the amphitheater.

A friend of Anicetus who witnessed a triumphal procession in Rome pointed out that the pompa is like the triumph. The only difference is that it is Storax, rather than the triumphant general, who leads the procession, and that it is the gladiators, hunters, and

▼ **Storax Presiding Over His Games.** Composed of three blocks of marble, this truncated pediment must have been positioned above the long frieze of paired gladiators, forming the decoration of the tomb building (fig. 62). The largest figure, in the center, is Storax, sitting on an elevated chair near the center of the platform. Two wide columns behind locate the scene in Teate's Forum. To his right and left are two pairs of men wearing togas who must be the four higher magistrates.

63 ABOVE Monument of Storax, Chieti. Detail, left part of the pediment. Straight-horn players, three attendants, and a group of four agitated fans

64 OPPOSITE, TOP House of the Labyrinth, Pompeii. Graffito on a column in the peristyle

65 OPPOSITE, BOTTOM Necropolis of the Nolan Gate, Pompeii. Graffito from Tomb 14 EN

condemned criminals who take the place of the regular soldiers, auxiliaries, and war prisoners. In both cases, it is a celebration of the sword—of prowess in dealing death. Blood will definitely be spilled.

It is a loud procession, with martial music provided by the horn players playing the same tunes to which the Roman army marches. The long-horn players lead the musicians, wearing colorful tunics and holding their instruments high. The curved-horn players follow, and a chorus of singers follows them. Next comes a display of the local smith's guild. The smiths are proud of the beautiful helmets, greaves, and swords they make for the hunters and gladiators, so they have constructed a float, a wooden litter that six of the guild members carry. On it stands a tableau with painted

wooden statues showing the smiths at work while Vulcan, their patron deity, looks on approvingly.

When the procession reaches the amphitheater, Storax mounts a wooden platform and gives a short speech thanking the city council for allowing him the honor of offering the games. He follows the prescribed order in naming his benefactors and friends, from the current city counselors down to the freedmen, and, in that same order, each steps forward to receive a sack of coins. The heaviest sacks go, of course, to those of the highest ranks. This giving of gifts precedes the games proper.

Now Anicetus, happy with the contents of his money sack, mounts the stairs to his section of the amphitheater, and Storax finally gives the signal for the games to begin.

A Fight Breaks Out. In this section of the relief a group of agitated fans are about to get into a fight (fig. 63). The only female figure in the relief is a woman in a V-necked dress who gesticulates in alarm as the three men start a brawl. This slice-of-life vignette may record one of the many fights that were apt to break out at the games—some of them turning into full-scale riots like the one recorded in the painting from Pompeii (see fig. 66). Storax probably included the scene to show the "common people" enjoying themselves, since the rest of his tomb relief show only officials and their ministers.

Graffito. Asteropaeus, the winner (V = *vincit*) is on the left; Oceanus, who was let off (M = *missus*), is on the right. Note that Oceanus is left-handed (fig. 64).

Fight Statistics. On the side of a tomb in Pompeii's cemetery, by the Nolan Gate, someone recorded four-day games given by M. Cominus Heredus of Nola (fig. 65). The inscription gives the statistics of three gladiators: Princeps, from Nero's gladiator school, fought twelve fights and won this one, as does Hilarus, who has fought fourteen fights and won this one. Creunus, who has fought six times, loses this one but is let go rather than killed. The enthusiastic graffitist has represented the musicians as well: curved-horn players and perhaps a drummer to the left, straight-horn players to the right.

▲ ▶ **A Riot in Pompeii's Amphitheater**
(fig. 66). Despite its distortions of conven-
tional perspective, the painting accurately
records architectural details of Pompeii's
amphitheater and the adjacent gymnasium
(*palaestra*) where the gladiators trained
(fig. 67). The inscriptions on the walls of
the palaestra trumpet two generous patrons
of the games of the Neronian period
(A.D. 54–68): D. Lucretius Valens and his
father, D. Lucretius Satrius Valens. The
crowd has descended from the bleachers
and, instead of professional fighters, men
with their tunics cinched up around their
waists run around gesticulating or engaging
others one-on-one. The battle thickens,
with several paired fighters between the
amphitheater and the palaestra. At the top
right, between the palaestra and the city
walls, the artist repeats the grisly image of a
man on the ground with a sword-wielding
adversary standing over him. Fighting is
thickest inside the amphitheater, on the
arena floor, where five men battle it out.

Remembering the Riot

N. Popidius Successus, freedman of Numerius, watches gleefully as his friend, the picture-painter *Fabius*, creates an unusual new picture for his little enclosed garden. It is a secret that he wants only his friends to know about, since it depicts what was for many—mostly the Nucerians, but also some Pompeians—a dark day in the history of Pompeii. Successus and his friends—all members of his now-suppressed gladiatorial fan club, the Campanians—still talk about it in excited whispers when they see each other on the street. This evening, in the privacy of Successus' house, they will celebrate it over dinner and wine. Best of all, in addition to members of the Campanians, Severus, one of Pompeii's most famous gladiators, will be in attendance. He has won fifty-five fights in his brilliant career, and has won his freedom.

It is almost five years since the event. For nearly 200 years, the inhabitants of Nuceria had come to Pompeii for the games, for Pompeii boasted the oldest and biggest amphitheater in the area. But relations between the two towns had become increasingly strained, especially after Nuceria grabbed the lands near Stabiae on which Pompeii depended for farming and grazing cattle. It was high time the ordinary people of Pompeii taught their bossy neighbors a lesson, so when Livineius Regulus, ex-Senator from Rome, announced that he was putting on a big day of games to build up his esteem in Pompeii—having made enough trouble in Rome to be exiled by Emperor Claudius—the Campanians and several of the other gladiator clubs got together and talked about revenge. The talk was mostly that—no real plan came out of it—but eventually it was decided to humiliate the

66 OPPOSITE House I, 3, 23, Pompeii. Peristyle n, west wall. *Riot in the Amphitheater*

67 BELOW The Amphitheater, Pompeii

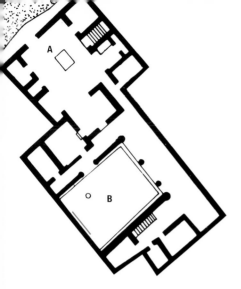

68 ABOVE Plan of House I, 3, 23,
Pompeii. Red indicates position of
the lost paintings of gladiators

69 OPPOSITE, LEFT House I, 3, 23,
Pompeii. Peristyle n, west wall.
Drawing of lost painting of
gladiators to left of *Riot*

70 OPPOSITE, RIGHT House I, 3, 23,
Pompeii. Peristyle n, west wall.
Drawing of lost painting of
gladiators to right of *Riot*

Nucerians with verbal abuse. During
the hunts in the morning, every animal
would be a Nucerian: "the wild boar from
Nuceria," "the Nucerian ostrich," "the
Nucerian camel." Just beneath those
taunts, though, Successus knew there
was real homicidal anger. And he also
knew that all the Campanians, at least,
were coming to the amphitheater armed.

Well, it didn't take long for the verbal
abuse to turn to stone-throwing, for the
stone-throwing to turn into fistfights,
and for the fistfights to turn into sword
fights. The games didn't go very far that
day. The professional hunters fled the
arena, herding the last of the unkilled
animals into cages. The noonday execu-
tions of condemned criminals didn't
take place that day—the dead were
victims of the bloody fights that took
place all the way down from the bleachers
into the arena and out into the area
around the amphitheater. The gladiators
stayed out of it. After all, they were
professional fighters, trained at great
expense in gladiator schools. They were
the expensive property of their owners
and didn't strain a muscle except for
their owners' profit.

The Nucerians were the big losers,
unprepared as they were for the fight. By
the time it was all over, Successus and his
friends had seen more blood and more
maimed bodies than after any game. They
saw grief-stricken Nucerians carrying

their dead and wounded back to Nuceria,
and even the Campanians themselves
mourned the loss of several members
of their fan club. Successus remembers
seeing a graffito on a house over near
the Forum addressed to his very own fan
club: "Campanians, although victorious,
you died along with the Nucerians!"

No wonder the Roman Senate stepped
in—at the order of Emperor Nero. The
trial was speedy and decisive. Livineius
and some of the worst offenders were
punished with exile to the far reaches of
the Empire. No games were to be held for
ten years, and—worst of all—all the fan
clubs were dissolved forever. It was
awful—the games had been the one thing
that made life in Pompeii worth living.

But now five years later, it looked as
though the games might return. There
was talk in the city council of getting an
imperial pardon, of the games starting
up again next year—with strict checking
of weapons at the gates, of course, and
special police to make sure there was no
rioting. The clearest sign that the ban
was unofficially lifted was the work going
on to repair the damage caused to the
amphitheater by the earthquake last
February. Successus himself had to
repair his little enclosed garden, and
that's when he decided to commission
Fabius to create the big painting of
the riot. Things were looking up for the
games at Pompeii.

◀ ▲ **A Modest House with a Subversive Painting.** The man who commissioned the *Riot* painting for his modest house made sure that it was well out of the sight of clients or casual visitors (fig. 68). In fact, the tiny atrium (A) makes it unlikely that the owner was rich enough to have clients visiting him. Flanking the big *Riot* painting on the west wall of the enclosed garden (B) were paintings of the end of a combat. In both cases, it is a Samnite about to deal the death blow to a fallen Thracian (figs. 69 and 70).

71 LEFT Sestertius of Titus/
Vespasian Divus, A.D. 80–81,
showing the Colosseum filled
with people. To left: the obelisk-
fountain (Meta Sudans). To
right: a portico

72 RIGHT House of the Vettii,
Pompeii. *Cupids Racing with Deer
Instead of Horses*

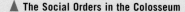

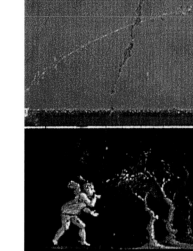

▲ **The Social Orders in the Colosseum**
(fig. 71). This official representation, on a coin circulated throughout
the Empire, shows the very order
that is upset in the *Riot* picture.
The Senators are in the bottom section with the Emperor's box in the
middle, the equestrians in the next
section up, followed by a section for
citizens, and then the highest tier
for slaves, foreigners, and women.

▶ **The Excitement of the Circus**
(fig. 72). The chariot races were
grand events, and the charioteers
enjoyed the same popularity as did
skilled gladiators. There were four
racing teams, or factions, each with
its distinctive color—the Blues, the
Greens, the Reds, and the Whites—
and people cheered on their favorite
teams. The race was dangerous, both
for the charioteers and the horses,
since it was such a long race—the
seven laps added up to 2.7 miles
(4 kilometers). In the painting, the
artist shows a chariot taking a spill—
a decisive moment for the race and a
favorite theme in art.

The Tavern of Salvius

It's A.D. 70, and life in Pompeii has almost returned to normal. Although many of the big buildings are still lying in pieces, awaiting repairs, *Primus* and *Secundus* are content with their new lives as manumitted slaves. They're both freedmen of the same mistress, *Vibia*, wife of the super-rich decurion Gnaeus Alleius Nigidius Maius. Primus and Secundus have been lovers for years— and neither Vibia nor Nigidius seem to mind, since the two men do their jobs so well. Primus has made Nigidius plenty of money by managing his real estate. At the moment, he's in charge of renting out spaces in the huge apartment block to the northwest of the Forum that Nigidius bought from Arrius Pollio.

Secundus is the valued personal slave— "No, now I'm a freedman!" he reminds himself—of Vibia. And what a lot of work she is! Secundus has given up actually *doing* Vibia's hair, or her wigs, or her clothes, or her makeup. He just directs the poor slaves who have to get every curl in place (and she has masses of them) and paint her to look like Aphrodite herself (or a common whore, in some peoples' opinion).

It's a holiday, a day of great theater— there was even a famous pantomime from Rome. Now it's time to visit their favorite haunt: Salvius' tavern over by the House of the Vettii. But something is awry when they walk in. Everyone's eyes are following them—all the regulars and a crowd of newcomers as well. Where's Salvius? Where's that bad-tempered waitress who calls herself *Amazonia?* Everyone starts to giggle, then they break out in laughter. Primus glances at the wall and sees that there's a new decoration. Four pictures in a row, something like the ones in the tavern across from the Fountain of Mercury. Dear gods! There's a picture of him and Secundus trying to get Amazonia to give them a pitcher of wine!

Secundus immediately sees that the artist—despite his modest talents— got their hairdos right, at least—long hair gathered up in a sort of bun. And they do wear their tunics a little long. Good heavens—he even got the color of his favorite gown! Not to mention Amazonia. For one thing, this woman is about twice their size. For another, she is about twice as tough; She could crush them with one arm—but sarcasm is her favorite weapon.

Primus, who's the better reader, intones the dialogue, while Salvius, their friends, and even Amazonia huddle around. Oceanus, who always brags about his exploits, is beaming. He thinks he's the star of the show. Primus and Secundus, secretly pleased by all the attention, grasp each others' hands, sit down, and get a whole pitcher of wine from Amazonia—on the house.

73 Tavern of Salvius, Pompeii. Scene 2, *Two Men and a Barmaid*

▼ Making Light of a Gay Couple.
The sharp contrast between the two men in this vignette and the men in scenes 1, 3, and 4—as well as their difficulty in controlling the huge, surly barmaid—suggest that the artist is depicting a gay couple (fig. 73). They are vying for the server's attention, one saying "Here!" *(Hoc!);* the other shouting "No, she's mine!" *(Non, mia est!).* Unfazed, the waitress replies "Whoever wants it, take it" *(Quis vol sumat),* but then has a change of heart, offering the wine to the beefiest character in the bar, the gladiator Oceanus: "Oceanus, have a drink" *(Oceane veni bibi).* A less literal translation might be: "OK, big boy . . . come and get it."

74 RIGHT Tavern of Salvius,
Pompeii. Room a, north wall. Four
scenes of tavern life, Naples
Archaeological Museum

75 BELOW Tavern of Salvius,
Pompeii. Scene 1, *A Man Kisses a
Woman*

▲ ▶ **Talking Pictures in Salvius'
Tavern.** The four comic vignettes
found in the tavern belonging to a
certain Salvius depend for their
humor on the lines of speech written (in really bad Latin) above the
characters' heads. The whole frieze
(removed at the time of excavation
in 1876) consists of four pictures
(fig. 74). In the first vignette, a
man kisses a woman while saying "I
don't want to ____with Myrtalis any
more" *(Nolo cum Myrtalis ____)*
(fig. 75). Although the verb is miss-
ing, it seems clear that the viewer
has inadvertently become a voyeur,
looking in on the beginnings of a
new romance. To make this funny,
the artist must have re-created the
portraits of a well-known couple—
regulars at the tavern or perhaps
celebrities of Pompeii. The third
and fourth vignettes go together to
form a little story (figs. 76 and 77).
Two men dispute the dice throw.
The man on the left, dice-cup in his
right hand, says "I won" *(exsi),* but
the other man disagrees, saying "It's
not three; it's two" *(non / tria duas /
est).* In the following scene, the
men come to blows, exchanging
insults. The man on the left says
"You no-name. It was three for me. I
was the winner." The other responds
"Look here, c********r. I was the
winner." *(noxsi / a me / tria / eco /
fui) (orte fellator / eco fui).* The
innkeeper wants none of this. He
tells them, "Go outside and fight it
out" *(itis / foras / rixsatis).*

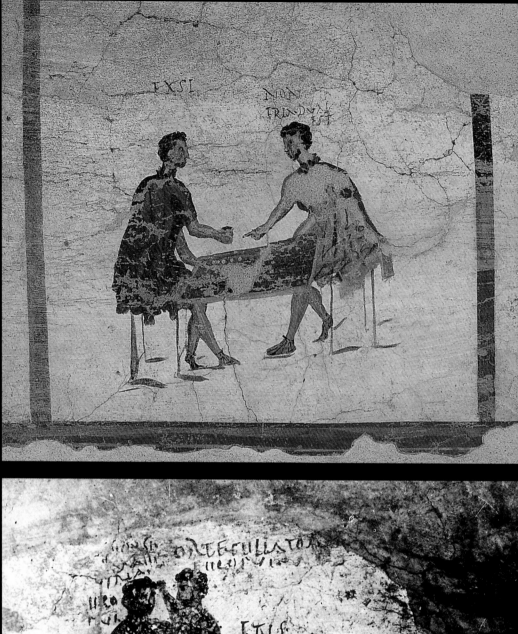

The Tavern of the
Seven Sages

Gamus, a counter from the Guild of the Grain Measurers, decides it's high time his friend, the brawny stevedore *Epaphroditus*, had a drink at his favorite tavern. Both men have been working hard all day, unloading grain from one of P. Aufidius Fortis' big ships. The stevedores, grain measurers, and counters have been working overtime; they've got to get all three ships unloaded and in Fortis' warehouse by the end of the week, or else there will be a penalty.

The Seven Sages is over in the new district, not far from the grain measurers' Guild Hall (see fig. 25). Gamus and Epaphroditus walk down the narrow alley flanking the big, brick-faced apartment building and quickly find the entrance, since a lot of customers are lolling about the doorway, wine cups in hand. Epaphroditus is impressed: The tavern is much bigger than he expected. The ceiling of the first room has a high barrel vault, and he can just see two more rooms like it behind. No mistaking that it's a place to drink wine. In fact, looking up, Gamus sees that the artist has made the vault into a kind of wine-heaven, with painted wine amphoras like the ones he often unloads, filled with wine from Spain and Gaul (fig. 78). The amphoras sit upright on tripods, and they're labeled. Epaphroditus can't read very well, so he asks Gamus, who tells him that he won't be tasting these wines tonight. One label says "falernum"—a very expensive wine from Campania.

There are more pictures of amphoras below, and then a row of fancy-looking men seated on four-legged stools. Some hold scrolls, others long staffs. There's some writing in Latin letters above their heads, and then two words in Greek letters to either side of the stools. At first he can't see the figures painted at the base of the walls because of the crowd of drinkers, most standing and milling about. But soon a dice game in one of the inner rooms heats up, and the room clears. Epaphroditus smiles, then he begins to laugh. The artist has painted a latrine around the walls of the room, with at least twenty men seated side-by-side, busily chatting as they relieve themselves! But there's a lot of writing above their heads, too, and he's at a loss. He again turns to his smart friend Gamus for help.

Gamus, who learned to read and write Greek and Latin from his parents, is delighted to show off his skills. First he reads the Greek labels on either side of the seated men: Solon of Athens, Thales of Miletus, Chilon of Sparta, and so on, informing Epaphroditus that these are the Seven Sages. In fact, Epaphroditus remembers seeing statues like these in the lecture hall at Ostia's Forum Baths— and he even remembers the famous saying of Thales: "Know thyself!" But he can see that there are too many words written above Thales' head to say "Know thyself." He presses Gamus to read it for him, and with a straight face Gamus intones:

76 OPPOSITE, ABOVE Tavern of Salvius, Pompeii. Scene 3, *Men Playing Dice*

77 OPPOSITE, BELOW Tavern of Salvius, Pompeii. Scene 4, *Dice Players Getting Into a Fight*

78 BELOW Tavern of the Seven
Sages, Ostia. Barrel-vaulted ceiling
with wine amphoras and a
Dionysiac flying figure

79 OPPOSITE Tavern of the Seven
Sages, Ostia. South and west walls

Durum cacantes monuit ut nitant Thales—
"Thales advised those who shit hard to
really work at it." Epaphroditus can't
suppress his laughter, and urges Gamus
to read all the Sages' maxims. Every
one of them is a commentary on bowel
movements—all cleverly written to
sound like fine poetry.

The lines of speech next to the pictures of the men sitting at the latrine are
hardly poetry. Just the opposite. They are
the kinds of things you might actually
hear while you're relieving yourself.
Every man in the bar had heard the likes
of these snippets of digestive wisdom—
the truest one being: *Amice fugit te
proverbium / bene caca et irrima medicos*
("Hey buddy—don't you know the saying?
If you shit well—to hell with the doctors—
you don't need them.") "Truer words
were never spoken," says Gamus.
It's time to get some food and drink.

▶ **Sitting Sages and Defecating
Commoners.** This barrel-vaulted
room, decorated around A.D. 100,
was one of three vaulted rooms,
lined up one behind the other, that
made up the large tavern (figs. 78
and 79). Only about a third of the
painting scheme survives, found by
the excavator beneath a layer of
white plaster that covered the paintings when the room became part of
a later bath in A.D. 130. Only three
of the Sages (along with the label
for a fourth) and only the heads of
four of the sitting men survive—
enough, however, to reconstruct the
original program (fig. 80). Luxury
latrines with numerous seats side-
by-side attest to the Roman habit of
defecating in common (fig. 81).

80 ᴏᴘᴘᴏsɪᴛᴇ Tavern of the Seven Sages, Ostia. West wall and ceiling

81 ʙᴇʟᴏᴡ Tavern of the Seven Sages, Ostia. Graphic reconstruction

82 ABOVE Latrine on the Street of
the Forica, Ostia

83 OPPOSITE Tavern of the Seven
Sages, Ostia. Detail of the west wall.
Chilon and the Sitting Men

▲ **Making Fun of Intellectual
Pretensions.** The paintings in the
Tavern of the Seven Sages get their
humor through role reversals. The
revered Sages say silly things about
bowel movements in poetic meter;
the real men below are all common
sense and street wisdom. By putting
the Sages on their philosopher's
stools and the men on a very different kind of seat—the latrine—the
artist reminds us that everyone—
Sage or commoner—defecates
(fig. 82). To get the jokes, a viewer
had to be able to read—or, like our
character Epaphroditus, have a friend
who could read for him. Although not
everyone could read, in a trade-and-
services city like Ostia, literacy must
have been fairly high.

► **The Sages' Sayings** (fig. 83). Above the first Sage, Solon of Athens: *Ut bene cacaret ventrem palpavit Solon,* or "To shit well Solon stroked his belly." Above the second Sage, Thales: *Durum cacantes monuit ut nitant Thales,* or "Thales advised those who shit hard to really work at it." Beneath Thales, who holds a philosopher's staff, is a fragmentary inscription that includes the words *(u)taris xylophongio,* or "use the sponge on wood." Since Romans used sponges to clean themselves after defecation, the phrase might suggest using the philosopher's staff for this purpose. Above Chilon of Sparta, pictured here: *Vissire tacite Chilon docuit subdolus,* or "Cunning Chilon taught how to fart without making noise." The men beneath him say: *propero,* "I'm hurrying up;" *agita te celerius pervenies,* "Shake yourself about so that you'll go faster;" and *amice fugit te proverbium / bene caca et irrima medicos* (see page 98).

VI

BATHS AND BATHING

A Visit to the New Baths

Petronia thinks that she will change her late-morning routine today. Instead of going to the old Forum Baths—her habit for most of her married life—she will venture through Pompeii's Forum and down the steep road that leads to the newly opened Suburban Baths. Her friend *Poppaea* tells her they are much more splendid than the Forum Baths. And, instead of having a separate, much smaller section for the women, they are unisex. That means, of course, that she and her women friends will have to use them in the mornings, when the men are busy seeing clients, but it also means that they will have the whole place to themselves.

Petronia orders her household slaves to ready her bathing things—what with sponges, skin scrapers *(strigils)*, perfumes, towels, and makeup, it is the work of two slaves to carry—and she orders her favorite black male slave, *Candidus*, to accompany them. She's pleased to see Poppaea herself at the entrance to the baths, paying a substantial but not unreasonable entrance fee. They enter the big exercise yard, where they see several of their friends huffing and puffing as they work out with hand weights to the shouts of a handsome Persian trainer

with a build like Hercules. Petronia and her retinue hurry to the dressing room, which is ringing with peals of laughter.

At first they don't get it. Why are the women at the back of the apodyterium doubling over with laughter? They've obviously just put their belongings into nicely made wooden boxes and placed them on the shelf that runs around the wall. Curiosity gets the better of Petronia, and she marches to the back of the room without even bothering to undress. There, she sees a naked woman speechless with laughter, pointing up at the very top of the wall, where she's just put her box, number IV. Squinting a little in the darkness, Petronia sees a shocking but very funny scene of a couple performing a taboo sexual act. She can't suppress her laughter either. In fact, all sixteen of the vignettes show outrageous sexual acts that no Roman woman would admit to doing! She and her friend Poppaea check them all out, and agree that it's a clever tactic on the part of the owner, a certain Crassus Frugus, to dispel the Evil Eye with healthy laughter. Very entertaining, and useful too. Now it's time to get some exercise and enjoy the two swimming pools everyone's raving about.

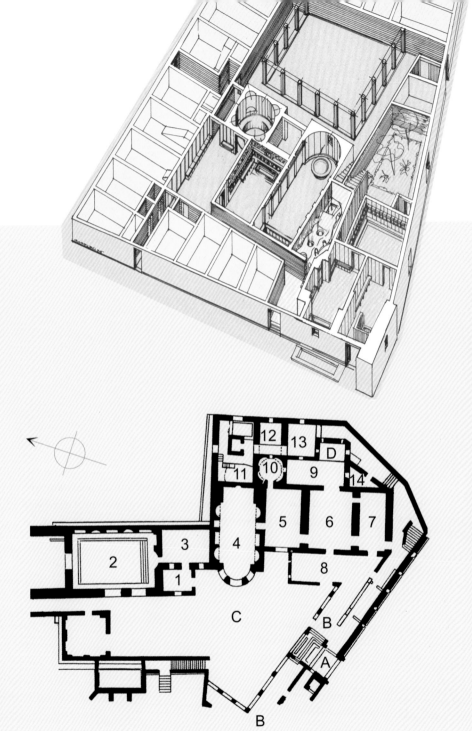

84 LEFT Forum Baths, Pompeii.
Plan. Women's rooms are in
pink, men's in blue

85 BELOW Suburban Baths,
Pompeii. Plan

◄ **Separate or Mixed Bathing?** Around the time the Suburban Baths were built (A.D. 40), the bath plan changes. Although the sequence of bathing stays the same—from dressing room (apodyterium), to exercise court (palaestra), through a series of increasingly hot rooms (tepidarium, laconicum, caldarium), to a plunge in a cold swimming pool (frigidarium)—builders no longer create separate rooms for men and women, as in Pompeii's Forum Baths (fig. 84). Pompeii's Suburban Baths lack these separate sections, leading some scholars to believe that men and women bathed together (fig. 85). Here I follow the more common opinion, that they used the same facilities but at different times of day.

86 Suburban Baths, Pompeii. Apodyterium. Digital reconstruction

◄ Laughter in the Dressing Room. This reconstruction of the dressing room of the Suburban Baths shows how the sexual vignettes worked (fig. 86). A bather—especially a beautiful woman or a handsome man—was highly susceptible to the envious gaze of other jealous bathers when undressing. Romans believed—as do many people today—that someone who envies your beauty can turn the Evil Eye on you, emitting particles that enter your body and make you sick or even kill you. Besides wearing amulets (often miniature phalluses or hands making an obscene gesture), people used paintings and mosaics that incited laughter. Everyone knew that it was impossible to focus the Evil Eye when the envious person or his victim was laughing!

87 BELOW Suburban Baths, Pompeii.
Mosaic waterfall

88 OPPOSITE Suburban Baths, Pompeii.
Frigidarium, painted decoration

▶ **Luxury Bathing.** The owner of the Suburban Baths took advantage of its two-story elevation to install a mosaic waterfall cascading into the smaller of the two swimming pools (9 on plan, fig. 85), an unheated cold plunge (fig. 87). Frescoes on the walls of the pool itself include fish and mythical sea creatures as well as warships of the Roman navy in combat (fig. 88). The other swimming pool was quite large and heated—another novelty for Pompeii (2 on plan, fig. 85). Excavators found a bronze boiler fueled by charcoal in room 11. Hot water circulated from the pool to the boiler and back again, to keep the pool at a constant temperature.

Emperor Hadrian's Gift to Ostia

Gaius Fulvius Victor, master mosaicist and freedman of Gaius Fulvius Salvius, climbs the vault painters' scaffold to examine his masterpiece. He has just completed the largest mosaic of his career, and he has reason to glow. It is magnificent! Little did he know when he started as an apprentice in the workshop of *Aemilius* that he would get a commission for the Emperor's new baths—or that he would be owner of the biggest mosaic workshop in Ostia.

When the Emperor decided to give the baths to Ostia, about fifteen years ago, this whole side of Ostia's main street—from the Forum all the way to the western city gate—was being demolished, filled in, and raised a good four feet (over one meter). Trajan's new harbor made Ostia into a boom-town, and new warehouses, apartment buildings, and baths had to go up fast. The only things that were saved were the venerable temples, preserved at the original, lower level.

In fact, Victor remembers the baths that were beneath these new ones; they, too, were decorated with elegant black-and-white mosaics. Now a new street runs over them, leading to the big barracks for the firemen that the Emperor built.

▼ **Neptune and His Retinue.** The Master of the Neptune Mosaic (whom I call Victor) is responsible for all the elegant mosaics of the Baths of Neptune (fig. 89). In this decorative program, created c. A.D. 125, the mosaicist created a united theme of mythic sea gods and hybrid marine creatures.

The Baths of Neptune (A), the Barracks of the Firemen (B), and the Insula of the Painted Ceilings (C) are all new structures built in A.D. 120–130 in the demolished quarter to the north of Ostia's Decumanus Maximus (fig. 90). The street to the east of the Baths of Neptune covers an earlier bath complex; archaeologists have unearthed an elegant black-and-white mosaic showing the Provinces and the Winds (fig. 91).

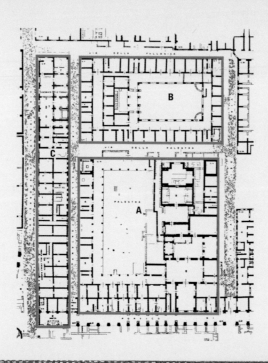

What matter? If the Emperor hadn't decided to devote a huge space to the new baths, Victor couldn't have let his fantasy have such full range. He decided—along with some help from the architect—to tell a story for the bather as he or she walked from room to room. With a plan of the building in hand, he began figuring it out. For the floor of the big dressing room, he sketched an image of Amphitrite riding a seahorse *(hippocampus)* with Tritons swimming around her along the edges. But in a moment of inspiration, he decided that she needed a guide in the form of little Hymenaeus, god of marriage. There she is—rushing at full speed through the doorway to meet Neptune, her future husband, in the great vaulted central salon.

Great indeed! This is the largest mosaic he or any of his workmen has ever laid: sixty by thirty-four feet (eighteen by eleven meters). He was, of course, able to use his model books to make one-on-one drawings for the workmen, to get the outlines right. About twenty years ago, he had decorated the much more modest baths of his friend Epictetus Buticosus with similar sea creatures. But this was the greatest challenge of his career—and one of which he is justifiably proud.

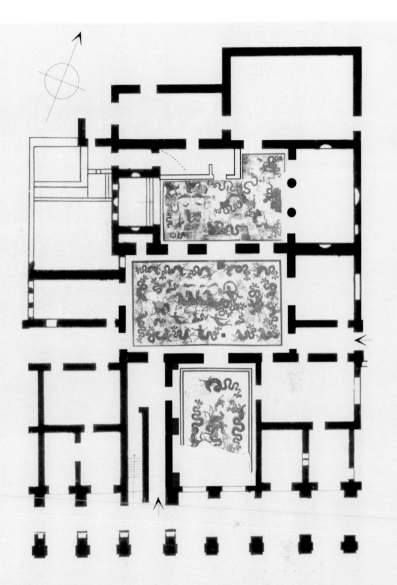

▲ **Marrying Amphitrite and Neptune with the Viewer.** In these aerial views the relationships among mosaics and architecture become clear (fig. 92). A viewer leaving the dressing room would follow the movement of Amphitrite, preceded by the god of marriage, Hymenaeus, to join Neptune. From that doorway, he or she would have the optimum view of the god of the seas speeding across the center, drawn by four hippocamps. The decoration of the frigidarium, with its twin cold plunge pools, seems off-center—until we realize that the figure of the sea monster Scylla is meant to be seen right-side up by someone passing between the two main doorways.

The Vettii Brothers' Dinner Party

Aulus Vettius Restitutus and his brother, Aulus Vettius Conviva, are having a conversation with *Syriacus*, their cook, surrounded by a dozen or so slaves. Tonight they will host a dinner party in honor of Gnaeus Helvius Sabinus, candidate for aedile; his wife *Cassia* will attend as well. If elected, Sabinus could further several of the brothers' schemes, including getting Aulus' son, now come of age, accepted into the order of the decurions. The other guests include Lucius Caecilius Iucundus and his wife, *Fabia*.

Since the weather is warm and there will be only the traditional nine diners, the brothers decide to have the three best bronze-and-wood couches set up in the "Ixion" room (fig. 93; see CD-ROM). They are particularly fond of the colorful, exuberant architectural perspectives, and the three big center pictures will provide some of the evening's entertainment. Conviva, the more studious

brother, reminds himself to study the subjects of the pictures—especially the two with Cretan myths—so that he can lead the conversation. Perhaps, if he has time, he will get his smart Greek slave, *Helios*, to help him work out a fancy picture interpretation to impress Sabinus.

As to the seating, it's clear that Sabinus has to be in the place of honor at the bottom of the middle couch. Fabia should be to his left, and to his right—well, that *is* a problem. The top place on the low couch is for the host, but since both brothers are hosting, should it be Restitutus or Conviva? Given Conviva's higher status as an Augustalis, Restitutus concedes the honor to his brother. Working out the other places is less difficult, except for the fact that there's no room for one of the brother's wives, but there is a tradition to cover this problem as well. Restitutus' wife, *Eutyche*, will sit on a chair at the end of the high couch.

93 House of the Vettii, Pompeii. Ixion Room

94 BELOW Diagram of seating in a
Roman dining room.

95 RIGHT Reconstruction of
dining Romans. Top: overhead view.
Bottom: eye-level view

▼ ▶ **Status and Reclining.** By the
time of the late Republic, Romans
had abandoned tables and chairs
for the Greek custom of dining while
reclining on couches. You immediately knew from the place assigned
to you how important you were in the
host's estimation (fig. 94). Normally,
there was space for nine persons on
three couches placed against the
right, rear, and left walls of a room.
On the right was the "high couch,"
at the rear the "middle couch," and
at the left the "low couch." The
guest of honor took his place at the
bottom of the middle couch, and the
Romans called this place of honor
the "consul's place." The host
reclined at the top of the low couch,
at the right hand of the guest of
honor. Strict etiquette surrounded
the ceremony of the Roman banquet.
Putting guests in the wrong place
could easily ruin a dinner party.

Where you reclined determined
what you got to see. The U-shaped
arrangement, along with the fact
that the guests were reclining,
meant that their gazes were focused
more than ours when we sit at the
table. The host and the guests on
the low couch looked across the
central table toward the right wall
and the entrance to the room;
the diners on the middle couch
faced toward the left wall and the
entrance; and those on the high
couch faced the guest of honor
and the host—and the imagery
on the left and back walls of the
room. The most important artwork
in a room—usually a complex
mythological picture—took pride
of place in the center of the rear
wall. Of course, during a long
evening, diners might shift positions
for a while, as you can see in the
artist's reconstruction (fig. 95).

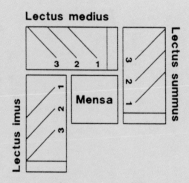

96 BELOW House of the Chaste Lovers,
Pompeii. Dining room g, west wall. *Couple
at a Symposium with Drunken Woman*

When the guests arrive, the brothers and their wives will greet them. Then the brothers' two handsomest Greek slaves, *Castor* and *Pollux*, will ceremoniously wash their feet before they take their places on the couches. For this special occasion, Restitutus and Conviva have added several ancient pieces to their silver service, and hope that Helvius Sabinus will notice the fine crystal goblets they have just bought—at a huge price. All Pompeii knows that Sabinus is a collector.

Weeks of planning have added a few gray hairs to the cook's head, but now—as he runs through the menu with Restitutus and Conviva—he is sure that his dinner will impress the guests. The appetizer course will begin with a variety of lettuces (as everyone knows, they relax the stomach) and wild mint to make everyone burp. Then there will be a series of delicate vegetables—baby leeks, arugula, squash, dark and light radishes—spiced with a variety of Pompeii's best fish sauces. Then will come three kinds of eggs (chicken, pheasant, and quail) cooked in three different ways (boiled, broiled in embers, and coddled), followed by anchovies garnished with hard-boiled eggs and fresh oysters. With this course, when little alcohol is called for, there will only be a heavy wine flavored with honey.

Syriacus, the cook, is particularly excited by the first dish of the first course: wild boar from Lucania. He has devised a special method of cooking it to make it tender, first soaking it in brine then boiling it. He will finish it by lightly grilling the cut-up pieces and garnishing them with wild onions and fava beans. The second dish is simpler but elegant: sow's udders in brine flavored with a tuna sauce. The wine is a light red from Sentinum, five years old.

The second course is lighter, abandoning the fruits of the earth for those of the air and sea. The first plates will feature birds tiny and large, from sparrows to blackbirds and pigeons. There will be a liver paté from a white female goose force-fed on figs. For the fruits of the sea, fish, mussels, clams, and mollusks; then plaice, turbot, and finally eel garnished with sea urchins. With this course the Vettii will serve a substantial red wine from the Greek island of Cos, ten years old.

For the dessert course, after the servants have laid new tablecloths and swept the floors, Syriacus's famous honey pudding will arrive, filled with dried fruits and chopped nuts. There will be plenty of fresh fruits and pastries as well. It will be a culinary masterpiece from beginning to end—"from the egg to the apple," as the Romans like to say.

Restitutus and Conviva are both secretly congratulating themselves for acquiring

◄ **Silver, Crystal, and Social Status.** The Romans prized fine tableware, as this painting of an ancient silver collection from a tomb demonstrates (fig. 97). Crystal goblets were even more expensive. The super-rich Vedius Pollio hoped to impress the Emperor Augustus with his crystal service. When a slave accidentally broke a priceless goblet, Pollio ordered him thrown into his fish tank to be eaten alive by huge lampreys. Augustus, outraged by his cruelty, ordered the slave saved—and forced Pollio to smash all his crystal and to have the fish pond filled in.

Syriacus: There will be no fault in the food. They are a bit concerned about the drinking party that will follow, for they have to make sure they choose the right guest to be master of ceremonies. He will be in charge of overseeing the toasts, the entertainments—and above all the mixing of the wine. Too much wine mixed with too little water will ruin a party. No one—especially their bibulous friend Jucundus—should get too drunk too soon, or the party will be spoiled. Arguments—or worse yet, sexual flirtations—might develop.

It's up to the "king of the banquet" to keep things on an even keel, from the moment when the guests put their banqueters' garlands on their heads and make

the first libation to the god Dionysus to the last toast of the evening. The brothers decide that they can trust their guest of honor, Sabinus, with the task.

This evening, the brothers have decided to dispense with the usual entertainers—the mimes, jugglers, and dancers—in favor of more highbrow amusements. Their sons' Greek tutor, *Ascyltos*, will read his new poem, "Ariadne's Lament," composed in response of the paintings in the Ixion room. These paintings sum up a key moment in the history of faraway Crete. (figs. 98, and 99; see CD-ROM). With the last lines, Ascyltos has already planned how he will turn—with a dramatic gesture—to the painting showing

101 OPPOSITE House of the Vettii, Pompeii. Dining room n, north wall. *The Infant Hercules Strangles Serpents Sent by Hera*

102 LEFT House of the Vettii, Pompeii. Dining room n, east wall. *Pentheus Torn Apart by the Maenads*

103 BELOW House of the Vettii, Pompeii. Dining room n, south wall. *The Punishment of Dirce*

the abandoned Ariadne rescued by Dionysus. It will be a perfect ending— and the right moment to toast the savior-god once again.

Then, Conviva will be able (if not too drunk) to wax philosophical about the connections among these paintings and those of the twin dining room at the other side of the peristyle (fig. 101, 102, and 103; see CD-ROM). Perhaps the guests will follow him in a tipsy procession to the other room, with its three pictures representing the mythical foundations of Thebes. Just in case, Conviva orders the slaves to set up three couches in that room as well. It promises to be a perfect banquet.

104 House of the Chaste Lovers, Pompeii. Dining room g, view from south window

▶ **Those Misbehaving Greeks!** The three paintings that decorate this elegant dining room use well-known models (two of the paintings appear in near-exact copies elsewhere). They depict the pleasures and perils of the Greek-style drinking party *(symposium),* where prostitutes *(hetairai)* entertained the men (fig. 104). In contrast to the Roman convivium, wives were not invited to the Greek symposium. Each picture sets up a different comic story. The picture on the east wall shows two hetairai about to get into a fight over a drinking contest (fig. 105). The male friend of the hetaira on the right has passed out, but the companion of the woman on the left is still barely conscious. To prove that he has won the drinking contest, this hetaira holds up her partner's head to squirt a bit more wine into his mouth from the drinking horn. On the rear wall we see two couples under a canopy (fig. 106). At the left sits the impudent female pipe-player. She has gone on strike, put down her double pipes, and is having a big drink. The couple next to her is getting intimate. In the third painting, a drunken woman, propped up by a servant, holds out her cup. She wants "one for the road."

105 OPPOSITE House of the Chaste Lovers, Pompeii. Dining room g, east wall. *Two Couples at a Symposium*

106 LEFT House of the Chaste Lovers, Pompeii. Dining room g, north wall. *Two Couples at an Outdoor Symposium Under a Canopy*

107 ʙᴇʟᴏᴡ House of the Moralist,
Pompeii. Triclinium 12

108 ᴏᴘᴘᴏsɪᴛᴇ House of the
Triclinium, Pompeii. Room r,
west and north walls, showing
the original positions of the
removed center pictures

► **Minding Your Manners?** Instead of
pictures, this garden dining room
has instructions on banquet behavior
painted on its walls (fig. 107). As
guests climbed up on the masonry
couches to take their places, they
would have read the pictures in
sequence. 1: "Let water wash your
feet, and let a slave boy dry them; Let
a napkin cover the couch; Don't dirty
our upholstery." 2: "Keep your sexy
looks off the other man's wife and
don't make eyes at her; Let modesty
show in your face." 3: "Refrain from
insults and avoid harsh quarrels if you
can, or else you go right back home."
Considering that the owners of this
house were former slaves themselves, it
is unlikely that they meant their guests
to take these commands seriously.
They are jokes aimed at their former
masters—the upper-class people they
had to take care of when they themselves were servants. How many of
the men and women who reclined in
this modest dining room had had to
carry home a drunken dinner guest
like the servant in fig. 96?

Marcus Casellius
Marcellus' Memories

Now that M. Casellius Marcellus is an old man, he gives few dinner parties. Yet whenever he misses what his stamina and his ailing health can no longer allow, he contents himself with a modest lunch in his lovely dining room—sometimes all alone, sometimes with his wife or one or two old friends (fig. 108). Years ago, while still in his prime, he had the talented picture painter *Nymphius* record his favorite evenings of feasting—each with a special meaning for him. This afternoon, the slaves have set up a lunch for two, so that his young wife (his adored *Euhodia* passed away some years ago) will have to listen once again to tales of days gone by.

109 RIGHT House of the
Triclinium, Pompeii. Room r,
east wall. *An All-Male Drinking Party*

110 OPPOSITE House of the
Triclinium, Pompeii. Room r,
north wall. *Male-Female Couples
Drinking*

Before he married, Marcellus recalls,
like many young Romans of his class he
preferred all-male drinking parties with
lots of handsome slave boys for entertainment (fig. 109). Nymphius has pictured one of the best, the one where his
friend Lucius Ovidius (father of Lucius
Ovidius Veiento, current candidate for
aedile) couldn't make it out of the triclinium to vomit, and a pretty slave boy
had to hold his head and clean up the
mess in front of everybody. But he's
placed this little incident off to the side.
The masculine beauty of the other diners
comes through. "What's this?" Marcellus

asks himself. He notices that someone
has scratched captions on the picture!
Above the heads of that couple on the
left, *Secundus* and *Magnus*, he's written
"I know" *(scio)*, and over the head of that
young boy on the right who's looking out
he's written "I'm drinking" *(bibo)*. But
over his own image the graffito reads
"Hello, everyone" *(valetis)*. Marcellus
doesn't much mind. "No harm done—
maybe it even livens up the picture." He
looks again at his own image so many
years ago, with his jaunty green mantle
pulled over his head (to hide his incipi-
ent baldness), his favorite black servant

turning to him while he gazes at a handsome boy in a white mantle whose name he has forgotten.

It's a very different moment that Nymphius has immortalized on the north wall, and one that Marcellus remembers quite well: that party where he met the love of his life, his much-missed Euhodia (fig. 110). They were well into the evening, and drinking ever-stronger wine, when Euhodia (the woman on the left) raised her drinking horn and—just as skilled as any man—squirted a perfect gulp of wine into her mouth with nary a drop escaping. Her companion, one of

the sons of C. Cuspius Pansa the elder, was too drunk to admire her skill, but Marcellus did. And just as in the picture, he turned from his own unexceptional dining partner and gave her his most seductive look. She said: "Make yourselves comfortable, I'm going to sing" *(facitis vobis suaviter, ego canto)*, and Marcellus replied: "That's right! To your health!" *(est ita, valea[s])*. It was, in fact, love at first sight, and the beginning of a long, loving marriage. He made sure to get the artist to write those words plainly on the picture. But this is not a story to tell his new wife.

The Right to Have a Public Face

Lucius Caecilius Jucundus has returned in haste from the house of his friend Aulus Vettius Restitutus, since it's time for him to open his own house to clients. Jucundus congratulates himself on the good taste that his father and grandfather (he is the third to bear this name) showed in the decoration of their house. The atrium and tablinum still have their original floors and wall paintings of the refined style of the time of Emperor Augustus. He, of course, has added to its splendors, only recently annexing the house next door and redoing the rooms around the back garden that suffered earthquake damage. In fact, to make sure there are no more earthquakes, he commissioned the sculptor *Heraklios* to carve a relief, showing the damage, to adorn his big Lararium. Each morning, when he dutifully sacrifices to the Lares and Penates of his house, he adds prayers and offerings to the Lares and Penates who protect Pompeii (see fig. 33).

But the noblest objects in his house are the two bronze portraits on either side of the entrance to the tablinum. They take the time-honored form of the herm: Rectangular pillars of marble, adorned only with bronze genitals, support the bronze portrait head (the genitals refer to the fertility of the Caecilius clan). When Jucundus stands there to receive his clients—as he will in a moment—he has the support of his ancestors. This is something that the Vettii brothers, for all their wealth (even now that Conviva is an Augustalis), cannot have, for they carry the stain of slavery. True, Jucundus' family, the Caecilii, doesn't go back so far in Pompeii—at least not so far back as the Holconii, the Popidii, or the Poppaei—but they are a solid family, any hint of former slavery in the now-distant past. And while Jucundus doesn't have any wax ancestor masks hanging in his atrium, he does have these fine bronze portraits recording every wrinkle and mole on his ancestors' noble faces.

111 OPPOSITE House of the Menander, Pompeii. Lararium 25, west wall. Shrine to ancestors and Lares

112 LEFT House of L. Caecilius Jucundus, Pompeii. Bronze herm portrait.

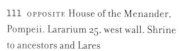

◄ **Verism and Wax Masks.** The Greek historian Polybius (writing around 130 B.C.) described the use of wax masks of illustrious ancestors in Roman funeral rituals (Polybius, *The Histories*, 6.53.4–6). When a member of an important family died, the family carried these masks to the funeral and put them on men who looked like the originals; these men donned the clothing and symbols of office of the ancestors to remind everyone of the family's importance and to inspire the young men of the family to seek further glory for the family. Amedeo Maiuri, excavator of the grand House of the Menander at Pompeii, claimed to have found the impressions of two miniature ancestor busts in a shrine. Finding hollows in the volcanic material, he poured plaster-of-Paris into the cavities. The casts that emerged were clearly two Lares and—less clearly—two miniature busts (fig. 111).

Although none of these masks survive, elite Romans had bronze and marble portraits made for display in their homes, like the bronze herm portrait, one of two that originally flanked the entrance of the tablinum in the atrium of the House of Caecilius Jucundus (fig. 112). The surviving portrait is highly realistic and unflattering, emphasizing—like the ancestor masks—Jucundus' age and no-nonsense character. This is a style of Roman portraiture known as verism. The inscription on the herm says: "From Felix to our patron Lucius." Felix was a slave or freedman of Lucius Caecilius Jucundus.

113 LEFT Villa of the Mysteries, Pompeii. "Rufus est" caricature from north wall of atrium

114 OPPOSITE House VII, 3, 30, Pompeii. Tablinum. *Bread Dole*

A Baker's Moment of Glory

The baker *Lucius Albucius Tiro*, freedman of Lucius Albucius Celsus, is considering how to improve his son Marcus' prospects for getting on Pompeii's city council. Although he has the support of his patron and former owner, currently running for the office of aedile, Tiro's social standing is modest at best. But in addition to buying his own freedom he owns his own bakery now—one of several that he ran for his former master. With the feast of Ceres, the baker's patron deity, coming up, the perfect move at this time would be to announce a bread dole for all free citizens of Pompeii. It would be easy to get the permission of the city council to distribute bread on the feast day. After all, times have been tough since the earthquake. Aid from Rome has been slow in coming, and too little at that. In addition to the production of his own bakery, he could lean on Celsus for help. Tiro still oversees a dozen or so mills and bakeries owned by his former master, and each could contribute loaves (for a discounted price) for his bread dole.

▲ **A Caricature of a Noble Roman.** Someone visiting the fine villa known as the Villa of the Mysteries outside Pompeii left a reminder that veristic portraiture had its down side (fig. 113). Since it emphasized a person's physical peculiarities, like baldness or a big nose, it easily became the subject of mocking graffiti. This one shows Rufus (possibly one of the proprietors of this grand villa) with a thin laurel crown that barely hides his baldness and with a big, bulbous nose.

▶ **A Bread Dole Picture in a Private House.** Discovered in a modest house in Pompeii in 1864, this painting has often been misidentified as a scene in a bakery (fig. 114). However, composition, clothing, and gesture emphasize the differences between the giver and the receivers. Unlike sales scenes, such as the relief of a saleswoman from Ostia (see fig. 50), where the counter allows direct exchange between buyer and seller, the artist has constructed a "dole station" to show the abundance of bread and the separation between the donor and the group of two men and a boy in the lower left. The man above is probably wearing a toga, which contrasts sharply with the dark tunics with hoods that the two men wear. Gestures also emphasize the ceremonial nature of the scene. The man giving out the bread is seated and calm as he reaches toward the man with the yellow cape, whereas the boy's jubilation is clear. The owner of the house commissioned this self-portrayal to record his moment of civic glory—probably a scheme to increase his civic importance.

▼ **A Grain Dole for All to See.**
Naevoleia Tyche's cenotaph on the
Herculaneum Road at Pompeii trum-
pets her virtues and those of her husband (fig. 115). This is not her tomb,
but rather the burial place for the
couple's freedmen and freedwomen,
erected to display her portrait and to
list—in the extravagant inscription—
the honors given to her husband, the
freedman Gaius Munatius Faustus.
But even if a viewer could not read,
he or she could see how important
Naevoleia and her husband were.
Naevoleia herself looks out of a
shuttered window at the top of the
inscription. Below it, we see ordinary
men, women, and children, some
carrying baskets, approaching a figure who is scooping grain from a
sack into a basket. On the right,
Munatius Faustus, dressed in a toga,
oversees the dole. Carved on the left
side of the monument is the double-
width theater seat (the *bisellium*),
which is one of the honors men-
tioned in the inscription: "Naevoleia
Tyche, freedwoman of Lucius,
[erected this monument] for herself
and for Gaius Munatius Faustus,
Augustalis and Paganus, to whom the
decurions, with the agreement of the
citizens, decreed the [honor of the]
bisellium for his merits. Naevoleia
Tyche constructed this monument
while alive for her freedmen and
freedwomen and for those of Gaius
Munatius Faustus."

Moral Lessons
for Children

Tiro has been on the receiving end of more than one such dole—and he knows how much glory the investment can bring to a freedman. He remembers, years ago, standing in line at the Forum while the wealthy freedman Gaius Munatius Faustus gave out wheat. Citizen men, many with their children on their shoulders and their wives at their sides, filed in, one by one, to get their baskets of grain. For this—and other donations—the decurions awarded Faustus a double-wide seat in the theater. He rose to become the representative of one of Pompeii's biggest wards, and a few years before his death the Emperor Nero made him an Augustalis. Everyone can see all of this—and read it—on the big tomb that his wife, Naevoleia Tyche, erected on the Herculaneum Road.

It's time now to start canvassing the city counselors and chatting up his friends. He'll visit his former master tomorrow morning at daybreak. Perhaps Tiro will commission a painting of the event for that empty spot on the wall of his little tablinum, so that everyone who visits him will remember the great day. But now there are many preparations to be made.

Marcus Lucretius Fronto, Junior, and his sister *Lucretia* are having their reading lessons in the little room next to the tablinum this morning so that their tutor, the severe but kindly *Phosphoros*, can demonstrate how to interpret pictures. The children have often wondered about these pictures, so they've looked forward to this lesson. The one thing they know is that in this room an artist painted portraits of their father and their aunt when they themselves were children. Their father was dressed up to look like the messenger god Mercury; aunt *Matidia* looked like Diana, goddess of the hunt (figs. 116 and 117). Lucretia certainly liked Diana, especially since she and a troupe of her girlfriends went to visit a sanctuary of Diana in the country and become Bear-Maidens—an old custom imported from Greece, her mother said. They dressed like Diana in short hunting tunics, slept in tents, and even learned to shoot a bow and arrow.

Phosphoros clears his throat and begins reciting verses from Ovid telling the story of Narcissus, the picture on the left wall (fig. 118). This is a story the children already know quite well: how

the handsome youth Narcissus spurned
the love of the beautiful nymph Echo—
all because he stupidly believed that the
image he saw in the water's reflection
was another beautiful boy. He died,
pining away for an illusion. "What, then,
is the moral of this story?" Phosphoros
asks the inattentive Marcus, who rescues
himself from his reverie by making up
an answer that basically says: Vanity kills.
Phosphoros adds a note: "And the gods

punish with death he who resists the
power of true love."

The picture on the south wall is some-
what worn away and has a lot of writing
on it (fig. 119). This is a tough one for
Marcus and Lucretia, for no matter how
hard they try, they can't get the verses
quite right. After leading them through
the Latin and explaining the poetic meter
and the origins of some of the words,
Phosphoros tells the tale of Pero and
Micon. Pero is the loving daughter who
visits her father, Micon, condemned
to starve to death in prison. Pero wants to
save him, but the only way she knows how
is to feed the old man with milk from her
own breast:

> *What food the mother*
> *was accustomed to offer to her newborns,*
> *unkind Fortune turned to*
> *food for her father.*
> *It is a task fit for eternity. Look*
> *how the slender veins*
> *of the old man's neck grow*
> *large with the flow of milk.*
> *Pero herself draws her face close*
> *to Micon and caresses him;*
> *a sad sense of shame together*
> *with piety is present.*

Both the children begin to understand:
This is piety toward your parents—the
highest virtue a Roman can have after
piety toward the gods. "And after all,"
thinks Marcus, who will inherit this house
one day, "we are Lucretii, the best family
in Pompeii. We're nothing if not pious."

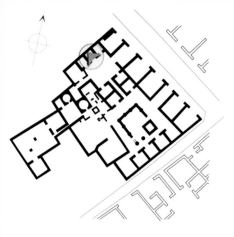

The Baker and
His Wife in the Bakery

If Lucius Albucius Tiro has arrived at the point of thinking about civic honors and giving out free bread, Terentius Neo and his wife *Timele* are contemplating a double portrait for the best room of their tiny house. It is not a proper house, but one annexed to the bakery that they run (fig. 120). Where to put it? They really don't have a tablinum, because they have no clients to receive—their "clients" are really the slaves who run in and out of the couple's living quarters from the bakery. So why not fix up the room at the end of the long corridor to the bakery? That's the room where he and Timele are most likely to be found, resting or doing accounts. Agreed. Neo has already asked the wall painters who are plastering and painting their few good rooms whether one of them can do a good double portrait. None of them can oblige, but they recommend a certain *Tertius*, saying he could produce a nice likeness for a modest price.

Tertius arrives the next morning with a sample book in one hand and a sketchbook in the other. Timele and

Neo examine Tertius's samples with amazement. To show that he can do a likeness, Tertius shows them paintings of the Emperor Vespasian and the Empress. And there are some other portraits of literary types: a woman looking up from the wax tablets she's writing on, her stylus held up in thought; a man with a big scroll in his hand. This is how they want to be depicted, they decide. It's not exactly truthful, since Timele can only read numbers and do simple arithmetic, and Neo's reading skills don't go much further than gladiatorial programs and tomb inscriptions. But why not upgrade their image?

The chief wall painter, *Agapitus*, has a great idea. He will put Cupid and Psyche above the double portrait (fig. 121). They will be embracing—a symbol of the couple's eternal love. Timele and Neo discuss the size of the painting and its price. Tertius begins sketching their portraits, once Neo changes into his toga (he is a freedman, after all) and Timele into her best red gown. Tertius will take care of the rest.

120 ABOVE House and bakery of "Terentius Neo," Pompeii. Plan with the position of double portrait marked

121 OPPOSITE House of "Terentius Neo," Pompeii, Room g, upper zone. *Cupid Embracing Psyche*

122 OPPOSITE House of "Terentius Neo," Pompeii. Room g. *Portrait of a Man and His Wife*

123 BELOW House at VI, 15, 14, Pompeii. Mosaic inset. *Portrait of a Woman*

The Rarity of Realistic Portraits. This double portrait found in a house annexed to a bakery in Pompeii melds the stock types of the "philosopher" and the "woman poet" with a realistic—even unflattering—rendering of facial features (fig. 122). This lack of idealization suggests that they are portraits of specific individuals. In style, the portraits closely resemble the mummy portraits from the area of the Fayum in Egypt. The only other portrait from Pompeii to convey the same kind of attention to nonideal traits of a person's face is much earlier—a mosaic portrait of a woman executed around 100 B.C. (fig. 123). It is made of tiny mosaic stones imitating brushstrokes. Note the irregularity of the woman's features and the attention to unusual details of her face and jewelry.

IX

DEATH AND FAME

Mulvia Prisca's Son

A.D. 73

It is the two-year anniversary of the death of her firstborn son, Gaius. When Mulvia's husband died, she and all the members of the Vestorius family pinned their hopes for civic glory on Gaius; they triumphed when he became an aedile at the early age of twenty-two. But in that same year he died, and with him, the Vestorius family lost their claim to glory.

Mulvia remembers her son's funeral as if it were yesterday. Gaius died at home of a terrible fever, surrounded by his family. Mulvia herself washed his body and dressed him in his toga; the servants placed him on a funeral couch in the atrium, with his feet facing the door. The perfume of flowers and incense filled the room. Pine branches around the doors announced that death had visited their house. Friends and fellow council members filled the atrium and followed the funeral procession: musicians first, followed by singers intoning dirges, and then Mulvia herself, leading the extended family (familia)—blood relatives, freedmen, and slaves. A long line of friends—including many of the decurions—followed the familia. There were the traditional torchbearers—even though it was day.

Mulvia listened and watched as her second son, Secundus, read a eulogy from the speakers' platform in the Forum of Pompeii. Secundus was just sixteen, and had only recently come of age, assuming the man's toga. Though the list of his brother's accomplishments was not long, the sincerity of Secundus' grief brought many mourners to tears. There were speeches by Gaius' fellow aediles and by several city counselors, then the sad procession proceeded to the place of cremation. Mourners covered Gaius' body with spices and perfumes, with gifts and love tokens. Secundus himself lit the pyre, his face averted as custom dictated. Then all there was to do was to keep herself steady until the fire burned out and the priest sprinkled purifying water over the mourners three times. At that point, all but the immediate family left: Gaius's tutor, Hymenaeus, gathered Gaius' ashes, and they shared a simple meal. On their return home, the family offered a pig to the Lares to purify their home.

The long "Nine Days of Sorrow" that followed were made even more difficult because Mulvia had to find a temporary resting place for her son's ashes in a tomb belonging to a family member. Another branch of the Vestorius family had a niche in a collective tomb (*columbarium*) on the Herculaneum Road. Mulvia returned to the cremation place with her son, her brother-in-law, and Hymenaeus to transfer Gaius's ashes in a fine cameo-glass jar. With bare feet and loosened belts, they carried the ashes to the tomb. The Nine Days ended, as custom dictated, with a sacrifice and a dinner in the house.

Although the specified time for mourning was ten months (the length of the ancient year), Mulvia decided to continue to wear black until today, when Gaius's ashes would rest in a fitting tomb. In the meantime, she and the family had visited Gaius during the memorial days (the *Parentalia*, February 13–23) and had brought him violets in March and roses in May. Mulvia made many visits to the decurions, for she was determined to build a fine tomb

▼ Augustus and His Heirs. One of the most impressive monuments in the city of Rome was the huge cylindrical mausoleum built by Augustus for himself and his heirs (fig. 124). It announced—along with the other monuments in the Field of Mars discussed in chapter 1, fig. 2— that Augustus was founding a new dynasty: that of the Julio-Claudians. The first ashes buried there were those of Augustus' nephew, Marcellus, in 23 B.C.; the last, those of the flamboyant Emperor Nero (A.D. 68). The immense brick-and-concrete structure became a fortress in the twelfth century, and later saw use as a bull ring in the nineteenth century. It was converted to a concert hall before becoming the archaeological centerpiece of the Piazza of the Emperor Augustus in the 1930s, when the site was opened as an archaeological landmark along with the newly moved and reconstructed Ara Pacis nearby. The restoration of the Mausoleum of Augustus to a place of prominence featured in Mussolini's ambitious reordering of the city of Rome, which strove to connect the aspirations of fascist Italy with the glories of the Roman Empire.

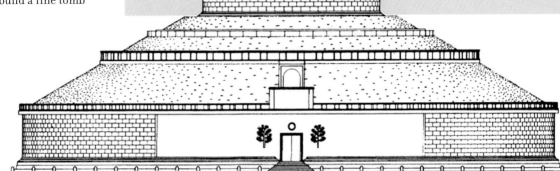

◀ ▲ ▼ **Tombs for All to See.** Romans created streets of tombs to create "cities of the dead" *(necropoleis)* outside the walls of all their cities (burial within the city walls was forbidden). Rather than creating cemeteries set off from the noise and movement of life, they vied for the most public and visible plots, those closest to the city gates or at least in the first row of tombs along the principal road (figs. 125 and 127). For the Romans, obsessed with prolonging a person's memory in public, tombs were meant to be seen as often as possible and by as many people as possible. Tombs could take various forms: The semicircular bench *(schola)* encouraged passersby to sit and contemplate the titles and accomplishments of the deceased—carved on the back of the bench. Other tombs (like that of Vestorius Priscus) consisted of an enclosure wall with an altar rising up above it. In the area excavated around the Tomb of Vestorius Priscus we see a schola tomb with a column behind it and another consisting of a large column base (fig. 126). The vertical stone markers *(cippi)* define the property belonging to each tomb.

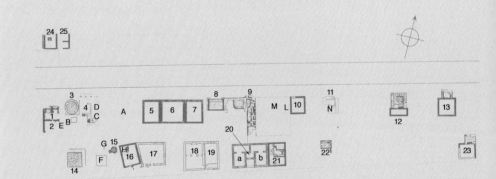

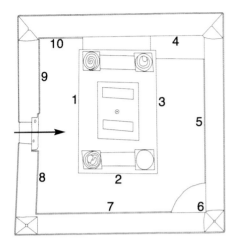

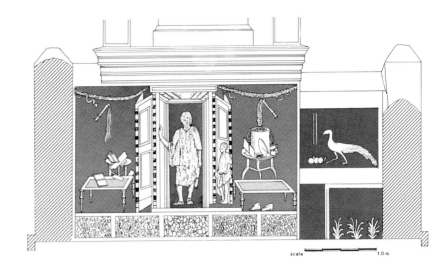

to commemorate her son's life. In the end, she persuaded the decurions to pay for Gaius' funeral and even to grant him a burial plot in an important space—right next to the Vesuvius Gate. Then she sacrificed all her savings to build the tomb itself.

Approaching the tomb today, Mulvia is relieved that there is no important spot left on the Herculaneum Road, because the tomb she was able to build would have been lost: It is not very large or imposing. Still, it makes up for its small size with the richness of its decoration. An altar rising above the enclosure walls now holds Gaius' ashes, and the inscription on its front tells who Gaius was and what Mulvia has done to keep his memory alive (fig. 128): "To Gaius Vestorius

Priscus, Aedile, who lived 22 years. This burial place and 2,000 sesterces for his funeral were given by decree of the decurions. His mother, Mulvia Prisca, paid for this tomb with her own money."

Mulvia is the first to enter through the little door at the back of the enclosure. The image that she first sees brings tears to her eyes: Gaius standing in the tablinum, dressed in his toga, ready to receive clients (figs. 129, 130, and 131). This was a duty he took over from his father. *Amulius*, the artist, has included all the details: the folding doors of the tablinum, the couches on either side, and even writing implements, scrolls, and coins on the table.

Moving to her right, Mulvia sees her son presiding over a merry banquet—a

128 OPPOSITE Tomb of Vestorius Priscus, Pompeii. Altar with inscription

129 LEFT Tomb of Vestorius Priscus, Pompeii. Plan with subjects and locations of paintings

130 RIGHT Tomb of Vestorius Priscus, Pompeii. Section showing Vestorius Priscus in his tablinum (scene 1) and garden plants and peacock (part of scene 5)

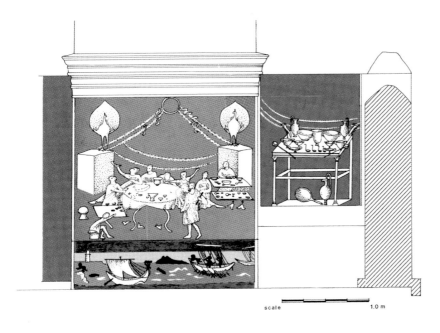

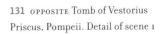

131 OPPOSITE Tomb of Vestorius
Priscus, Pompeii. Detail of scene 1

132 LEFT Tomb of Vestorius Priscus,
Pompeii. Section showing *Banquet*
and *Pygmies on the Nile* (scene 2) and
Table with Silver Service (scene 4)

133 BELOW Tomb of Vestorius
Priscus, Pompeii. Scene 2. Above:
Banquet. Below: *Pygmies on the Nile*

scale ——— 1.0 m

far cry from the sad Ninth Day meal
that ended the first period of mourning
(figs. 132 and 133). The men sit around
a circular couch under a huge canopy
with two statues of peacocks on pedestals:
Amulius has re-created their garden and
the banquet that celebrated Gaius' election
as aedile, and he's even added captions
above some of the banqueters' heads.
Looking down, Mulvia is not sure she
approves of the frieze of Pygmies that
Amulius placed at the bottom—but he
had assured her that in all the best tombs
his clients always included naughty

Pygmies to distract the evil spirits known
to lurk around tombs. These are harm-
less enough, Mulvia supposes, although
they're naked and the three on the boat
on the right are only dancing merrily.
What's this? Amulius has another Pygmy
leaning out over the shore to poop on
a fish. She laughs in spite of herself.
Like all intelligent people, Mulvia knows
that laughter dispels demons—so Amulius
was right.

  Moving once again to the right (for
one always circles a tomb in that direc-
tion), Mulvia sees the most important

Pompeii. Section showing *Priscus
and Twelve Attendants* (scene 3), with
altar above and gladiators on west
enclosure wall (scene 8)

135 OPPOSITE, TOP Tomb of Vestorius
Priscus, Pompeii. *Priscus with
Attendants* (scene 3). Detail

136 OPPOSITE, BOTTOM Tomb
of Vestorius Priscus, Pompeii.
Lead tube on top of altar

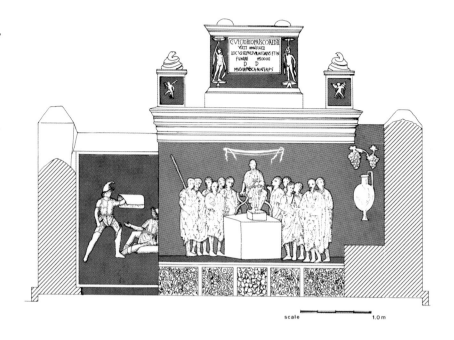

scale   1.0 m

painting of all, right beneath the inscription on the front of the altar (figs. 134 and
135). Although only the family members
will ever see this painting, it records for all
time Gaius' moment of glory, when he was
aedile and the town of Pompeii looked up
to him. There he is, seated in the chair of
his office (the *curule* chair) on the high
podium, surrounded by twelve men in
togas. This was Mulvia's son at the age of
twenty-two!

Mulvia instructs a trusted servant to
place two silver pitchers on the ledge
beneath the painting of the family's silver drinking service (see fig. 97). One
contains milk, the other wine. It is with
some difficulty that two servants maneu-
ver a ladder into position so that her son
Secundus can climb up to the top of the
altar and pour the libations into the tube
that flows to his brother's ashes. These

libations will appease the spirit of poor
Gaius (fig. 136). Since there is so little
space between the enclosure wall and
the base of the altar, Mulvia and her
sons and daughters slowly file out, looking at the other beautiful scenes that
Amulius has painted on the enclosure
wall: a garden with fountains and peacocks,
a wild-animal park, two gladiators, a
temple front with an open door, and
a pomegranate tree. Servants set up
a modest funeral picnic in back of the
tomb while the rest of the familia enters
the low door and look at the paintings,
some leaving offerings of incense, wine,
or food on the little ledges inside. Mulvia
takes her place on the small couch they
have brought for her. Finally her tears
have stopped—forever, she hopes.
She has immortalized her son, Gaius
Vestorius Priscus.

137 BELOW Necropolis on
the Laurentine Road,
Ostia. Plan, tombs 17–22.
The road runs along the left

138 RIGHT Necropolis
on the Laurentine Road,
Ostia. View of tombs of
Apella and his heirs,
from the east

139 OPPOSITE Necropolis of the Laurentine Road, Ostia. Interior of columbarium 18

140 RIGHT Necropolis of the Laurentine Road, Ostia. Tomb 22, south enclosure wall. Excavation photo

◀ ▲ Apella and His Heirs.

Excavations along the Laurentine Road leading south from Ostia revealed a group of four tombs—each of a different form—built by a freedman named Gaius Lucius Apella during the reign of Augustus, 27 B.C.–A.D. 14 (figs. 137 and 138). Inscriptions list the people who could legally be buried there. In addition to Apella's wife and his freed slaves, several persons not belonging to the familia are listed: These are either friends or individuals who bought places for themselves from Apella—a common practice. These four tombs continued to be used until about A.D. 150, when, like much of the city of Ostia, this necropolis was filled in and the level of the road raised so that new tombs could be built on top of the old ones.

Within Apella's tomb complex, the vaulted building is a typical columbarium—so named because the many niches of urns containing ashes resemble a dovecote (fig. 139). The open area of tomb 22 included a masonry dining couch for the banquets that commemorated the deceased (cut through by a later well) (fig. 140). The most important days for remembering the dead were the *Parentalia* (in February) and the *Lemuria* (in May), when families visited the tombs, cleaned them, and decorated them with wreaths and flowers. Former slaves or people without heirs often joined funerary societies that promised a proper burial and specific remembrances, such as the annual funeral banquet in honor of their members.

141 RIGHT Garden of the House
of the Doctor, Pompeii. Digital
reconstruction of Pygmy paintings

142 ABOVE Isola Sacra, near Ostia.
Tomb 16, black-and-white mosaic
in front of columbarium. *Pygmies
Surrounding a Head of Ocean*

143 OPPOSITE Tomb of Apella,
Necropolis of the Laurentine Road,
Ostia. Tomb 22. *Lion Devouring a Bull*,
with frieze of Pygmies boating below

◄ ▲ **Pygmies, Wild Animals, and Death.** The antics of naughty Pygmies frequently appear in tomb painting and mosaics—as well as in the decoration of gardens (figs. 141 and 142). They seem to have been both a reference to the exotic Nile and a charm against the evil spirits haunting outdoor spaces where people gathered to dine. The usual accompaniments to Pygmy scenes are images of the wild animal park, or *paradeisos.* The image of a lion devouring a bull or a cow from the Tomb of Apella has a frieze of Pygmies boating below (fig. 143; see also excavation photo, fig. 140).

144 Sarcophagus of
Trophimas with details,
Ostia

Remembering Trophimas

A.D. 150

Cremation Versus Inhumation.
Beginning in the second century A.D. Romans began to prefer interment in stone coffins *(sarcophagi)* over the practice of cremation and burial in ash urns. Sarcophagi, usually carved only on three sides, since they were placed against the interior walls of tombs, satisfied the patrons' desire to make a showy monument for the deceased. Most surviving sarcophagi, mass-produced in stone-carving centers like Aphrodisias in modern Turkey, repeat standard mythological scenes. Only a few, like the sarcophagus of Trophimas, present images specific to the deceased person's work, religious beliefs, or life story.

This morning, Claudia Apphias and her partner Lucius Atilius Artemas have a sad mission to accomplish. They are walking through Ostia's streets toward the workshop of the sculptor *Pyramus* to commission a sarcophagus for their dear companion, Titus Flavius Trophimas, who died after a brief illness at the age of forty-five. The three of them had been childhood friends, growing up in Ephesus. When one of them—was it Trophimas?—heard that there was plenty of work for ropemakers in the booming port city of Ostia, all three found passage on the same ship. That was over twenty years ago.

Trophimas and Artemas set up a little shop. Trophimas' trade was that of a ropemaker, and in a bustling shipping center, that was a skill in high demand. Artemas was a shoemaker. Claudia kept accounts. They had modest lodgings at first, above the shop; later, they bought a comfortable apartment in a new building nearby. Nothing was lacking; their only difficulty was mastering Latin—a clumsy language compared to their native Greek. With practice, they were able to communicate tolerably well—but with noticeable Greek accents. No matter—Ostia was filled with foreigners like them, and as

long as they accepted their noncitizen status and abided by the laws, they felt welcome. There were a lot of good times, like the many evenings when Trophimas, an accomplished artist, sang and danced for them. Best of all were the celebrations in honor of their cherished goddess Isis. The local priests quickly recognized Trophimas' extraordinary talent and made him leader of the sacred mimes who instructed initiates in the mysteries of the goddess. Now it was all over.

Claudia and Artemas arrive at the sculptor's workshop. He comes from Ephesus as well, like most of their friends. They talk of their beloved companion, tears streaming down their faces. Pyramus makes a most welcome suggestion: He could make a sarcophagus large enough for all three of them, so that in death—as in life—they could stay together. There will be images of Trophimas and Artemas at work and at play, with a big Greek inscription in the middle proclaiming Trophimas' virtues and the story of their happy life together (fig. 144). Pyramus sketches the composition. Claudia and Artemas are quite happy with the sketch of Artemas at work making shoes, with Claudia holding distaff

in his right hand while stretching rope
with his left arm. But Pyramus' rendition
of Trophimas dancing doesn't do justice
to his beautiful body and his grace as a
dancer. They suggest that the sculptor
give his muscles more emphasis, and put
him in a more revealing garment—perhaps
the loincloth he frequently wore. In a
stroke of genius, Pyramus puts the forked
sticks in Trophimas' hands—a musical
instrument of old Egyptian origin that
Trophimas often played to age-old
melodies. Next to him he puts his friend
Artemas, dressed in the transparent gown
of Isiac dancers (though usually worn
by the female dancers), and gives him a
tambourine to keep time to Trophimas'
expert dance steps.

They compose the inscription on
the spot, and their sad work is finished:
"We, Lucius Atilius Artemas and Claudia
Apphias, [dedicate this sarcophagus] to
Titus Flavius Trophimas, incomparable
and trusted friend, who always lived with
us. We have given his body a place to be
buried together with us, so that he will
always be remembered and will find
rest from his sufferings. The straightfor-
ward one, the cultivator of every art, the
Ephesian, sleeps here in eternal repose."

CONCLUSIONS

Seeing with Roman Eyes

This book has followed many Roman people through portions of their lives that we know about because of both ancient texts and archaeology. The stories of what each person did, whether sacrificing to the protector-deities of their houses, organizing a dinner party, or bringing a new baby into the world, show how the buildings, paintings, sculptures, and even the graffiti make best sense when we connect them to specific individuals and circumstances.

Whether it is the Emperor Augustus or the freedman Publius Clodius inaugurating an altar, the images carved on the altar spring to life because we know who instructed the artist to make them. When we look at the painting of the riot in the amphitheater through the eyes of someone who was part of that riot, it comes to life. If we put ourselves in Mulvia Prisca's place, we begin to understand why she crowded his little tomb with images of what her young son would have accomplished had he survived more than twenty-two years.

Self-representation takes on new meaning when we understand the pride that Verecundus and his wife took in their clothing shop, or the importance of showing all the employees hard at work in the fullery. So many of the images we've considered were commissioned by individuals who wanted to show themselves as they were. Humble activities like measuring grain, tending a shop, or having a drink with friends appear, as well as important moments in a person's life, whether it was sponsoring a lavish gladiatorial spectacle or giving out a dole of grain or bread.

Literacy in Roman Life

Humor, too, comes to life when we put real Romans in front of the images in the two taverns we've looked at. In the Tavern of Salvius, cartoonlike paintings with speech lines poke fun at hot-tempered dice-players who get ejected by the owner. In the Tavern of the Seven Sages, it's the ordinary drinkers who get to make fun of the intellectual pretensions of the upper classes. The fact that it is not just the images but also the writing that make these tavern paintings funny reminds us of the importance of written language in Roman life. If we put together these humorous captions with the great variety of inscriptions on tombs and civic monuments, we begin to understand that life in a Roman city encouraged literacy. Even if only a few mastered the complexities of poetry and philosophy, it seems that many ordinary people could read simple texts and inscriptions.

The House as a Power-House

This book has taken us into several homes at Pompeii, most notably that of Aulus Vettius Restitutus and his brother Aulus Vettius Conviva. Following Restitutus through part of his day, we come to realize that the Roman house was quite different from the modern home built around the notion of the nuclear family. The Roman house served a variety of activities that we locate outside the home: receiving business clients; housing a work force of slaves; worshiping the gods; mourning and burying the dead; entertaining on a lavish scale. The Roman house was an expression of the owner's personal power and social status. Open to the public for a part of each day, the house and its decorations told the city who you were and what you were worth.

If the house represented a Roman's wealth and status, its decorations ranged from complex mythological pictures to portraits. In the CD-ROM on the House of the Vettii, where you must assume a role to enter decorated rooms, it soon becomes apparent that the artist has hidden themes within the pictures that encourage viewers to show their knowledge of mythology. The paintings become part of after-dinner entertainment.

Personal Representations

The portraits of children in the House of Lucretius Fronto, juxtaposed as they are to the stories of Narcissus and Pero, encouraged the children of the household to speculate on moral themes: the price of vanity and the importance of filial piety. If the pictures of revelers in the House of the Chaste Lovers invited speculation about those naughty Greeks in the old days, the pictures of banquets in the House of the Triclinium showed the owner enjoying the company of high-spirited friends: "Make yourself comfortable. I'm going to sing," says one of them. The double portrait of Terentius Neo and his wife greeted workers and customers coming in from their bakery. In every case, these paintings—whether portraits or mythological images—spring to life if we think of them as part of the daily reality of the people who lived in the house.

Just Like Us?

We have looked at a cross section of Roman people, from the Emperors to the men who trod cloth in the wool-treating plants. The usual way of studying ancient Roman life assumes a kind of top-down or "trickle-down" model; scholars assume that what we read in the texts describes the whole of Roman society, and that what happened in Rome happened in all other cities of the Empire. Texts written by elite men, however, focus on men of their own class. They are silent about the people who wrote no literature: women, freeborn workers, slaves, and foreigners. It is only by studying visual representations that we can get to know these previously invisible Romans.

In the Introduction, I explained why the ancient Romans were *not* like us, and the many social practices we have come to know by looking at their art supports this idea. At this point, though, I can turn this statement around. If we understand the ancient Romans in all their diversity—of ethnicity, social standing, religious beliefs, language, and so on—they *are* like us in many ways. Because the Empire founded by Augustus was so successful, all Romans had to negotiate an increasingly complex cultural environment. Despite the appearance of social homogeneity that legal, military, and economic institutions projected, the reality was one of people of highly diverse cultural formation learning to live together in spite of their deep differences. This could be an accurate description of our own shrinking globe in the twenty-first century.

It is nothing short of a miracle that we are able to re-create ancient Roman life with such accuracy, thanks to the preservation of ancient cities like Pompeii and Ostia. Following so many different individuals through events in their lives, we begin to realize that—just like them—we construct our own ways of doing things, ways to negotiate the ups and downs of life. The value of thinking of the Romans as being like ourselves is that it leads us to ask better questions about our own practices, beliefs, and judgments.

Even if there are no set answers, these questions are important ones. They remind us that there are many ways of constructing the rituals of everyday life—whether today or 2,000 years ago. In other words, the stories we tell—about ourselves and what we do, about our heroes, about our families, our work, our recreation, about death—shape our lives in very real ways. These narratives often tell us how to act in a given situation. They constitute what we call culture. And it is these individual stories that eventually shape what we call history. Obviously, it is worth examining the stories we tell. In so doing, we have the possibility of understanding our lives and perhaps making them fuller, more open, and more enjoyable for ourselves and those around us.

GLOSSARY

aediles
Roman magistrates, elected annually, responsible for the care of the city

apodyterium
dressing room of a bath

atrium
central hall of the Roman house

Augustalis
member of a religious and social institution open to wealthy freedmen, who were otherwise legally barred from holding civic magistracies

auxiliary
noncitizen soldier recruited from a conquered district to serve in the Roman army; the auxiliary is distinct from the citizen-soldier, or legionary

barbarian
non-Roman, generally used of tribes opposed to Rome in battle

basilica
large, multipurpose public hall usually adjacent to a Forum

bisellium
seat in the theater or amphitheater of double width, awarded as a special honor

caldarium
hot room of a bath

censor
one of a pair of senior Roman magistrates entrusted with making up the official list of Roman citizens (*census*) and overseeing the morals of the community

cippus
upright stone marking a boundary

circus
Roman arena for chariot-racing

civium Romanorum
of, or belonging to, Roman citizens

cohort
fighting unit of 500 or 1,000 men

collegium
any private association of fixed membership; there were *collegia* organized around specific trades as well as *collegia* to carry out funerals

Colosseum
popular name for the Flavian Amphitheater in Rome, completed in A.D. 80

columbarium
Roman dovecote; also, a type of tomb so called because of its similarity to a dovecote, with niches arranged in rows in the walls for pots containing the ashes of the dead

consul
chief civil and military magistrates of Rome; two were elected annually to this highest office of the state

crypta
covered passageway or vaulted corridor, as in the theater at Pompeii

curule chair
ivory folding seat, without back or arms, used by the higher Roman magistrates

decurion
councilor who ran Roman local government in both colonies and municipalities; qualifications included wealth, age, free birth, and reputation

duumvir
chief civil and military magistrate of cities outside of Rome; two were elected annually

equestrian
a second aristocratic order which ranked below only the senatorial order in status

eunuch
castrated male

familia
group under the power of a paterfamilias, including the nuclear family, those sharing the *gens* (clan) name, former slaves, and slaves

fasces
bundles of elm or birch rods, about five feet long, and a single-headed axe, carried by *lictores*

Forum
an open square or marketplace in a Roman town, combining political, religious, judicial, and commercial functions

freeborn citizen
Roman born without the stain of slavery; children of freed slaves were freeborn

freedman/freedwoman
emancipated slave, called a *libertus/a* in relation to the former owner (*patronus/a*); *libertinus/a* in relation to the rest of society; slaves became Roman citizens upon manumission.

fresco
wall painting in which the pigment is applied to the wet plaster so that it is incorporated (carbonated) into the final plaster layer

frieze
any long horizontal band of ornament

frigidarium
cold room of a bath

fullonica
wool-treating establishment

gens
clan, extended family, relations under the power of the *paterfamilias*; all freeborn members of a *gens* bore the same name

gladiator
combatant at the games (*munera*); there were specialized fighting styles and weapons, as well as schools for training gladiators; gladiators suffered the status of infamy

haruspex
diviner; haruspices interpreted thunderbolts, unusual happenings, and the entrails of sacrificial victims

herald
Latin, *apparitor*; an official who attended magistrates and priests

herm portrait
portrait head atop a vertical shaft of rectangular section

hetaira
Greek term for a talented prostitute, not unlike the Japanese geisha

infamy
infamia, legal term limiting a person's civic rights for illegal or immoral activities; prostitutes of both sexes, actors, and gladiators suffered the status of infamy because they put their bodies on display

laconicum
superheated sweating room of a bath

Lararium
shrine to the *Lares* of a household or a city

Lares
twin deities, protectors of the home (*Lares familiares*) and of the crossroads (*Lares compitales*)

legionary
soldier recruited from the Roman citizenry; a legion comprised about 5,000 men; there were 25 legions in service in A.D. 14; 33 in A.D. 200

Lemuria
Roman private ritual on May 9, 11, and 13 to propitiate hungry ghosts (*lemures*) then prowling about the house

lictor
attendant or bodyguard of a magistrate; the *lictor* carried the *fasces*

maenad
female devotee of Dionysus, often represented dancing ecstatically

manumission
freeing of a slave; a properly manumitted slave received Roman citizenship

mausoleum
monumental tomb, often circular in plan

necropolis
literally, "city of the dead"; cemetery

obelisk
in Egyptian architecture, a slender squared monolith tapering toward a pyramidal top

obstetrix
midwife

palaestra
exercise court of a bathing establishment

pantomime
dance of an individual performer who conveyed specifics of character and plot solely through movements of his body

Parentalia
public religious festival dedicated to the commemoration of the dead, February 13–21

paterfamilias
male head of the *gens*, or extended family

patron
Latin *patronus/a*; owner of a slave; benefactor of a *collegium* or of a city

Penates
Roman spirits connected with the inner part of the house

peristyle
> covered, colonnaded walkway around a central courtyard or garden; the peristyle is a ubiquitous feature of the Roman house

pompa
> procession; especially the parade of gladiators at the beginning of the games, or *munera*

pontifex maximus
> chief priest of the Roman religion

portico
> porch; colonnade walkway

praetorian
> member of the *cohors praetoria,* guards charged with the protection of the emperor and members of the imperial family

priest
> man or woman of high rank, chosen for service of the gods and goddesses

princeps
> "first citizen," unofficial title chosen by Augustus

salutatio
> daily visit of clients to their patron's house

sarcophagus
> stone coffin

scaenae frons
> stage building of the Roman theater, decorated with columns, aedicules, and niches with statues

schola
> tomb of semicircular shape, often outfitted with a bench

Senator
> member of the most important political and social body in the Roman Empire

statio
> office; space of business

stola
> long garment worn by women

symposium
> Greek term for a drinking party

syncretism
> attempt to reconcile disparate, even opposing, beliefs and to meld practices of different religions

tablinum
> main reception room of the Roman house where the *paterfamilias* received clients and conducted business

taurobolium
> sacrifice of a bull, associated with the cult of Mithras and the cult of Cybele or Magna Mater; it could be a purification ritual for a devotee to be bathed in the blood of the bull

tepidarium
> lukewarm room of a bath

toga
> long wool garment, around twenty feet in length, worn by male Roman citizens

tribunal
> in the Roman theater, one of two elevated platforms to either side of the stage building

triclinium
> dining room outfitted with three couches (*klinai*)

verism
> style of portraiture that emphasizes lifelike rendering of the sitter's features—including all his or her flaws

vicomagister
> ward-captain; official in charge of a *vicus,* or ward, of the city of Rome; Augustus reorganized the *vici* in 7 B.C. and entrusted each to four *magistri,* who were usually freedmen

victimarius
> man responsible for killing the victim in a Roman sacrifice

FURTHER READING

Adkins, Lesley, and Roy A. *Handbook to Life in Ancient Rome*. New York: Oxford University Press, 1994.

Aldrete, Gregory S. *Daily Life in the Roman City: Rome, Pompeii, and Ostia*. Westport, Connecticut: Greenwood Press, 2004.

Carcopino, Jerome. *Daily Life in Ancient Rome: The People and the City at the Height of the Empire*. Second edition. New Haven, Connecticut: Yale University Press, 2003.

Clarke, John R. *The Houses of Roman Italy, 100 B.C.–A.D. 250: Ritual, Space, and Decoration*. Berkeley: University of California Press, 1991.

———. *Art in the Lives of Ordinary Romans: Visual Representation and Non-elite Viewers in Italy, 100 B.C.–A.D. 315*. Berkeley: University of California Press, 2003.

Connolly, Peter, and Hazel Dodge. *The Ancient City: Life in Classical Athens and Rome*. New York: Cambridge University Press, 1998.

Connolly, Peter. *Pompeii*. New York: Oxford University Press, 1990.

D'Ambra, Eve. *Roman Art*. New York: Cambridge University Press, 1998.

———. *Roman Women*. Cambridge Introduction to Roman Civilization. New York: Cambridge University Press, 2007.

Johnston, Mary. *Roman Life*. Chicago: Scott Foresman & Co., 1957.

Jones, Peter, and Keith Sidwell, eds. *The World of Rome: An Introduction to Roman Culture*. New York: Cambridge University Press, 1997.

Mau, August. *Pompeii: Its Life and Art*. New edition. New Rochelle, New York: Caratzas Brothers, 1982 (1902).

Meiggs, Russell. *Roman Ostia*. Second edition. Oxford: Oxford University Press, 1973.

Ramage, Nancy H. and Andrew. *Roman Art*. Fourth edition. Upper Saddle River, New Jersey: Pearson Prentice Hall, 2005.

Shelton, Jo-Ann, ed. *As the Romans Did: A Sourcebook in Roman Social History*. Second edition. New York: Oxford University Press, 1998.

Wallace-Hadrill, Andrew. *Houses and Society in Pompeii and Herculaneum*. Princeton: Princeton University Press, 1994.

Warrior, Valerie M. *Roman Religion*. Cambridge Introduction to Roman Civilization. New York: Cambridge University Press, 2006.

Zanker, Paul. *Pompeii: Public and Private Life*. Cambridge, Massachusetts: Harvard University Press, 1998.

LIST OF ILLUSTRATIONS

96. House of the Chaste Lovers, Pompeii. Dining room g, west wall. *Couples at a Symposium with Drunken Woman*. Photo by Michael Larvey

97. Tomb of Vestorius Priscus, Pompeii (A.D. 70–79). North wall, east part, scene four: *A Table Set with Antique Drinking Silver*. Photo by Michael Larvey

98. House of the Vettii, Pompeii. Dining room p, north wall (A.D. 62–79). *Daedalus Shows the Wooden Cow to Pasiphae*. Photo by Michael Larvey

99. House of the Vettii, Pompeii. Dining room p, south wall. *Dionysus Discovers the Abandoned Ariadne*. Photo by Michael Larvey

100. House of the Vettii, Pompeii. Dining room p, east wall. *The Punishment of Ixion*. Photo by Michael Larvey

101. House of the Vettii, Pompeii. Dining room n, north wall (A.D. 62–79). *The Infant Hercules Strangles Serpents Sent by Hera*. Photo by Michael Larvey

102. House of the Vettii, Pompeii. Dining room n, east wall. *Pentheus Torn Apart by the Maenads*. Photo by Michael Larvey

103. House of the Vettii, Pompeii. Dining room n, south wall. *The Punishment of Dirce*. Photo by Michael Larvey

104. House of the Chaste Lovers, Pompeii (IX, 12, 6–7). Dining room g, view from south window (A.D. 35–45). Photo by Michael Larvey

105. House of the Chaste Lovers, Pompeii. Dining room g, east wall. *Two Couples at a Symposium*. Photo by Michael Larvey

106. House of the Chaste Lovers, Pompeii. Dining room g, north wall. *Two Couples at an Outdoor Symposium Under a Canopy*. Photo by Michael Larvey

107. House of the Moralist, Pompeii (III, 4, 2). Triclinium 12 (A.D. 62–79). Soprintendenza Archeologica di Pompei. Archivio Fotografico degli Scavi 81032

108. House of the Triclinium, Pompeii (V, 2, 4). Room r, west and north walls, showing the original positions of the removed center pictures (A.D. 62–79). Photo by Michael Larvey

109. House of the Triclinium, Pompeii. Room r, east wall. *An All-Male Drinking Party*. Museo Nazionale Archeologico, Naples, inv. 120029. Photo by Michael Larvey

110. House of the Triclinium, Pompeii. Room r, north wall. *Male-Female Couples Drinking*. Museo Nazionale Archeologico, Naples, inv. 120031. Photo by Michael Larvey

111. House of the Menander, Pompeii (I, 10, 4). Lararium 25, west wall. Shrine to ancestors and Lares. Photo by Michael Larvey

112. House of L. Caecilius Jucundus, Pompeii (V, 1, 26). Bronze herm portrait of Caecilius Jucundus. Museo Nazionale Archeologico, Naples, inv. 110663. Photo by Michael Larvey

113. Villa of the Mysteries, Pompeii. "Rufus est" caricature from north wall of atrium. Drawing by Onur Öztürk

114. House VII, 3, 30, Pompeii. Tablinum e. *Bread Dole* (A.D. 62–79). Museo Nazionale Archeologico, Naples, inv. 9071. Photo by Michael Larvey

115. Necropolis of the Herculaneum Gate, no. 22, Pompeii. Monument of Naevoleia Tyche (A.D. 62–79). Photo by Michael Larvey

116. House of Lucretius Fronto, Pompeii (V, 4, a). Room c, west wall, north part. *Portrait of a Boy in the Dress of Mercury* (A.D. 62–79). Photo by Michael Larvey

117. House of Lucretius Fronto, Pompeii. Room c, west wall, south part. *Portrait of a Girl*. Photo by Michael Larvey

118. House of Lucretius Fronto, Pompeii. Room c, north wall. *Narcissus Contemplating His Own Reflection*. Photo by Michael Larvey

119. House of Lucretius Fronto, Pompeii. Room c, south wall. *Pero and Micon*. Photo by Michael Larvey

120. House and bakery of "Terentius Neo," Pompeii (VII, 2, 6). Plan with the position of double portrait marked. Drawing by Onur Öztürk

121. House of "Terentius Neo," Pompeii. Room g, upper zone. *Cupid Embracing Psyche* (A.D. 62–79). Museo Nazionale Archeologico, Naples, inv. 9195. Photo by Michael Larvey

122. House of "Terentius Neo," Pompeii. Room g. *Portrait of a Man and His Wife*. Museo Nazionale Archeologico, Naples, inv. 9058. Photo by Michael Larvey

123. House VI, 15, 14, Pompeii. Mosaic inset. *Portrait of a Woman* (100–50 B.C.). Museo Nazionale Archeologico, Naples, inv. 124666. Photo by Michael Larvey

124. Mausoleum of Augustus, Rome (27–20 B.C.). Hypothetical reconstruction. Drawing by Onur Öztürk

125. Necropolis of the Herculaneum Gate, Pompeii. View. Photo by Michael Larvey

126. Tomb of Vestorius Priscus, Pompeii (A.D. 70–79). Excavation photo, 1907, showing its context. Soprintendenza Archeologica di Pompei. Archivio Fotografico degli Scavi 280

127. Necropolis of the Ostia Road, Ostia. Plan. Drawing by Onur Öztürk

128. Tomb of Vestorius Priscus, Pompeii. Altar with inscription. Photo by Michael Larvey

129. Tomb of Vestorius Priscus, Pompeii. Plan with subjects and locations of paintings. Drawing by Onur Öztürk

130. Tomb of Vestorius Priscus, Pompeii. Section showing Vestorius Priscus in his tablinum (scene 1) and garden plants and peacock (part of scene 5). Drawing by Jane K. Whitehead

131. Tomb of Vestorius Priscus, Pompeii. Detail of scene 1. Photo by Michael Larvey

132. Tomb of Vestorius Priscus, Pompeii. Section showing *Banquet* and *Pygmies on the Nile* (scene 2) and *Table with Silver Service* (scene 4). Drawing by Jane K. Whitehead

133. Tomb of Vestorius Priscus, Pompeii. Scene 2: Above: *Banquet*. Below: *Pygmies on the Nile*. Photo by Michael Larvey

134. Tomb of Vestorius Priscus, Pompeii. Section showing *Priscus and Twelve Attendants* (scene 3), with altar above and gladiators on west enclosure wall (scene 8). Drawing by Jane K. Whitehead

135. *Priscus with Attendants* (scene 3). Detail. Photo by Michael Larvey

136. Tomb of Vestorius Priscus, Pompeii. Lead tube on top of altar. Photo by Michael Larvey

137. Necropolis of the Laurentine Road, Ostia. Plan, tombs 17–22 (20 B.C.–A.D. 150). Drawing by Onur Öztürk

138. Necropolis on the Laurentine Road, Ostia. View of tombs of Apella and his heirs from the east. Photo by Michael Larvey

139. Necropolis on the Laurentine Road, Ostia. Interior of columbarium 18 (c. 20 B.C.) Photo by Michael Larvey

140. Necropolis on the Laurentine Road, Ostia. Tomb 22, south enclosure wall. Excavation photo. Archivio Fotografico della Soprintendenza Archeologica di Ostia A 2249

141. Garden of the House of the Doctor, Pompeii (A.D. 62–79). Digital reconstruction of Pygmy paintings by Julianna Budding

142. Isola Sacra, near Ostia. Tomb 16, black-and-white mosaic in front of columbarium, *Pygmies Surrounding a Head of* Ocean (c. A.D. 150). Photo by Michael Larvey

143. Tomb of Apella, Necropolis on the Laurentine Road, Ostia. Tomb 22. *Lion Devouring a Bull*, with frieze of Pygmies boating below (c. A.D. 150). Photo by Antonio Ortolan

144. Sarcophagus of Trophimas, Ostia. Left: Ropemaking and Shoemaking; center: inscription; right; Two Men Dancing (c. A.D. 150–200). Rome, Museo Nazionale delle Terme, inv. 184. Photo by Michael Larvey

INDEX

Page numbers in italics refer to illustrations.

Editor: Margaret L. Kaplan
Assistant Editor: Aiah R. Wieder
Designer: Russell Hassell
Production Manager: Jules Thomson

Library of Congress Cataloging-in-Publication Data
Clarke, John R., 1945–
  Roman life : 100 B.C. to A.D. 200 / by John R. Clarke.
      p. cm.
   ISBN-13: 978-0-8109-9339-6 (hardcover)
   ISBN-10: 0-8109-9339-2 (hardcover)
 1. Rome—Social life and customs. 2. Rome—Religion.
 3. Rites and ceremonies—Rome. 4. Rome—Antiquities.
 5. Pompeii (Extinct city) I. Title.

  DG78.C577 2007
  937'.607—dc22   2007004398

Published in 2007 by Abrams, an imprint of
Harry N. Abrams, Inc.

Printed and bound in China
10 9 8 7 6 5 4 3 2 1

HNA

harry n. abrams, inc.
a subsidiary of La Martinière Groupe
115 West 18th Street
New York, NY 10011
www.hnabooks.com